I0426283

March 2012

DEFINED CONTRIBUTION PLANS

Approaches in Other Countries Offer Beneficial Strategies in Several Areas

GAO

Accountability ★ Integrity ★ Reliability

DEFINED CONTRIBUTION PLANS

Approaches in Other Countries Offer Beneficial Strategies in Several Areas

Highlights of GAO-12-328, a report to congressional requesters

Why GAO Did This Study

Service providers play important roles in the U.S. defined contribution (DC) retirement system since they provide services, such as administration and fund management, necessary for operating DC plans. Plan sponsors rely on such providers, yet it is unclear how much participants are paying in fees for these services. Other countries with well-established DC systems face similar issues and some use a variety of approaches to oversee DC plans and service providers and actively focus on fees charged to participants.

GAO was asked to examine, for selected countries' DC systems, (1) how are service providers overseen by regulatory agencies; (2) what key strategies are used to improve fee disclosure to participants; and (3) what key strategies are used to reduce fees? GAO selected Australia, Chile, Sweden and the United Kingdom based on, among other factors, the importance of the DC plans to the country's retirement system and the use of strategies to address service providers' fees. GAO reviewed research on DC plans; collected and analyzed available data; and interviewed government officials, pension experts, service providers, and other relevant representatives in the U.S. and selected countries.

What GAO Recommends

GAO is recommending that Labor consider other countries' experiences as it continues to improve its supervision and requirements related to fee disclosures. In commenting on a draft of this report, Labor generally agreed with the findings and noted that it will consider GAO's recommendations carefully.

View GAO-12-328. For more information, contact Charles Jeszeck at (202) 512-7215 or jeszeckc@gao.gov.

What GAO Found

In overseeing DC plans and service providers, regulatory agencies in the countries GAO reviewed use risk-based approaches to target practices deemed most likely to harm participants and to develop preventative measures. While the role of service providers varies, DC plans and service providers in the 4 countries GAO reviewed are overseen by multiple agencies—primarily a pensions regulator and a securities regulator. In each of these countries, the pensions regulator is the agency that regularly collects data on service provider fees, as well as other plan features, which are used to inform their oversight activities. In particular, in several of these countries, the pensions regulator uses these data as part of a risk-based approach to identify service provider practices that may harm participants, instead of relying only on a compliance-based approach. For example, in Chile, pensions agency officials evaluate key features of the DC system, such as the service providers' management of the individual accounts and the composition and role of the board of directors of the service provider. In both Chile and Australia, agency officials said using a risk-based approach enables the pensions regulator to take proactive measures to ensure the DC plans are operating in the best interest of participants. These countries have used risk-based approaches to oversee service providers for a number of years, while the U.S. Department of Labor (Labor) has just begun to develop a risk-based approach in its efforts to oversee U.S. DC plans and service providers.

Other countries have used key strategies to improve the disclosures participants receive about the fees they pay for their DC plans, including presenting disclosures in a consistent, summary format, which has increased transparency. In particular, these countries have made disclosures simpler and more uniform to facilitate comparisons, and one has required that providers highlight the long term impact of fees on participants' account balances. In addition, some countries require that participants receive personalized information about the total amount they pay in fees over a given time period. In Chile, participants not only receive personalized fee disclosures, but they also receive a statement that tells them what they would have paid had they chosen the lowest-cost option. Many of these requirements exceed Labor's disclosure requirements for U.S. DC plan participants.

Other countries use several targeted strategies—including consolidating and streamlining administrative services and establishing low-cost default funds—to keep the fees paid by their DC plan participants at reasonable levels. According to officials in the countries GAO reviewed, it was important to use these targeted strategies because many of their DC plan participants remain disengaged from retirement savings issues despite improved disclosures. For example, in Sweden and the United Kingdom, consolidating administrative functions eliminates the need for fund managers to maintain individual accounts. Representatives from service providers in both countries said this structure allows them to significantly lower their fees. In addition, for individuals who do not actively choose where to invest their contributions, some countries have established low-cost default options through a variety of measures, such as creating a nonprofit entity to run the default fund under a low-cost mandate, increasing the use of online services, and eliminating marketing costs. These countries also take other targeted approaches to lower fees, such as direct regulation of fees.

_____ **United States Government Accountability Office**

Contents

Figures

Abbreviations

AFP	*Administradoras de Fondos de Pensiones*
DB	defined benefit
DC	defined contribution
EBSA	Employee Benefits Security Administration
ERISA	Employee Retirement Income Security Act of 1974
GDP	gross domestic product
IOPS	International Organisation of Pension Supervisors
Labor	U.S. Department of Labor
NEST	National Employment Savings Trust
OECD	Organisation for Economic Co-operation and Development
SEC	Securities and Exchange Commission
U.K.	United Kingdom

United States Government Accountability Office
Washington, DC 20548

March 22, 2012

The Honorable George Miller
Ranking Member
Committee on Education
  and the Workforce
House of Representatives

The Honorable Robert E. Andrews
Ranking Member
Subcommittee on Health, Employment,
  Labor, and Pensions
House of Representatives

Service providers—companies that employers hire to provide the services necessary to operate defined contribution (DC) retirement plans, such as investment management, consulting and financial advice, recordkeeping, custodial or trustee based services for plan assets, and basic customer service—play an important role in the U.S. DC system. As employers who offer DC plans rely on these providers, whose fee arrangements are becoming increasingly complex, it is unclear how much participants are paying for their services. Because the amount of a participant's retirement savings in a DC plan depends on their investment rate of return net of fees, higher direct and indirect fees charged by DC plan service providers can significantly decrease the income available to participants in retirement. Furthermore, oversight of these companies has become more complex because their services and activities may fall within the jurisdiction of multiple regulatory agencies. In order to improve employers' abilities to adequately oversee service providers and monitor the fees participants are charged for their services, the U.S. Department of Labor (Labor) issued an interim final rule in 2010 to increase the transparency of direct and indirect fees in DC plans to plan sponsors. The final rule will go into effect in 2012, and its impact remains to be seen.[1]

Other countries with well-established DC systems face similar issues, and some use a variety of approaches to oversee DC plans and service

---

[1]Reasonable Contract or Arrangement Under Section 408(b)(2) - Fee Disclosure, 77 Fed. Reg. 5632 (2012) (to be codified at 29 C.F.R. pt. 2550).

providers and actively focus on fees charged to participants. Congress is interested in understanding what approaches other countries are using to address these issues compared to the approaches used in the United States. In particular, Congress is interested in whether U.S. regulators can benefit from learning about these alternative approaches as well as the challenges those countries encounter in utilizing and overseeing service providers in their DC plans. In light of this, you asked us to answer the following questions:

1. How are service providers in other countries' DC systems overseen by regulatory agencies?

2. What key strategies are used in other countries to improve fee disclosure to participants?

3. What key strategies are used in other countries' DC systems to reduce fees?

To answer these questions, we selected four countries in which to conduct case studies: Australia, Chile, Sweden, and the United Kingdom (U.K.). To select these countries, we initially reviewed scholarly and nonlegal sources describing the DC retirement systems in other countries. Based on our analysis of relevant research and interviews with pension experts, we identified 10 countries that had DC systems with key features designed to address fees. From those 10 countries, we established selection criteria based on the importance of the DC system to the country's retirement system and the use of strategies to address service providers' fees, among other factors. By focusing on countries in which the DC system is an important pillar of the retirement system, we increased our opportunity to identify practices used in countries with well developed capital markets and where risks to participants are comparable to those faced by participants in the United States. For each of the four countries selected, we reviewed research and other available documentation and interviewed officials and industry experts to determine the role that service providers play in these countries' DC systems and how they are overseen, and to identify the strategies designed to address fees. We obtained broad perspectives on the benefits and drawbacks of the identified strategies from government officials, academics, industry experts, service providers, and other relevant representatives in each country. Where possible, we attempted to obtain and analyze available data on the types and amounts of fees paid in DC plans in those countries. We did not conduct any independent legal analysis to verify the information provided by or about those countries laws or regulations.

Appendix I provides additional information on our scope and methodology.

We conducted this performance audit from March 2011 through March 2012 in accordance with generally accepted government auditing standards. Those standards require that we plan and perform the audit to obtain sufficient, appropriate evidence to provide a reasonable basis for our findings and conclusions based on our audit objectives. We believe that the evidence obtained provides a reasonable basis for our findings and conclusions based on our audit objectives.

Background

Roughly 40 percent of all U.S. workers participate in pension plans offered by their employers.[2] Under Title I of the Employee Retirement Income Security Act of 1974 (ERISA), employers are permitted to offer their employees two broad types of retirement plans, defined benefit (DB) and DC. Over the past three decades, there has been a general shift by employers away from DB plans to DC plans, the most predominant of which is the 401(k) plan. According to estimates by industry researchers, 51 million American workers were active 401(k) plan participants in 2010 and, by year end, 401(k) plan assets amounted to $3.0 trillion.[3] Unlike DB plans, employers that offer 401(k) plans do not promise employees a specific benefit amount at retirement—instead, the employee and/or the employer contribute money to an individual account held in trust for the employee.[4] Participants direct these contributions to mutual funds and other financial market investments; the amount available at retirement is dependent on, among other things, investment returns net of fees. In this way, 401(k) plan participants have more control over their retirement assets than DB plan participants but also bear the responsibility for ensuring they have adequate retirement savings.

[2] Employee Benefit Research Institute, *Employment-Based Retirement Plan Participation: Geographic Differences and Trends, 2010*, Issue Brief No. 363 (Washington D.C.: October 2011).

[3] Employee Benefit Research Institute, *401(k) Plan Asset Allocation, Account Balances, and Loan Activity in 2010*, Issue Brief No. 366 (Washington D.C.: December 2011).

[4] Exemptions to this trust requirement include insurance contracts and plan assets held by insurance companies.

Employers who offer these plans are considered plan sponsors and generally have the responsibility to act prudently and in the best interest of the plan's participants as they hire various outside companies to help run the plan and choose investment options to offer in the plan.[5] Most 401(k) plans allow participants to direct the investment of their contributions, but their choices are generally limited to those investment options their plan sponsor chooses to offer. Participants also pay a number of fees, including expenses, commissions, or other charges associated with operating a 401(k) plan.[6] Fees are charged by the various outside companies that the plan sponsor hires to provide a number of services necessary to operate the plan. Services can include investment management (e.g., selecting and managing the securities included in a mutual fund); consulting and providing financial advice (e.g., selecting vendors for investment options or other services); recordkeeping (e.g., tracking individual account contributions); custodial or trustee services for plan assets (e.g., holding the plan assets in a bank); and telephone or web-based customer services for participants. An investment company, bank, advisor, or insurance company may offer any or all of these types of investment products as plan options to a 401(k) plan. As shown in figure 1, service providers can be used to provide a number of services necessary to operate a 401(k) plan.

---

[5] 29 U.S.C. §1104(a). The law establishes that a plan fiduciary includes a person who has discretionary control or authority over the management or administration of the plan, including the plan's assets. Typically, the plan sponsor is a fiduciary under this definition. ERISA requires that plan fiduciaries carry out their responsibilities prudently and do so solely in the interest of the plan's participants and beneficiaries. In accordance with ERISA and related Labor regulations and guidance, plan sponsors and other fiduciaries must exercise an appropriate level of care and diligence given the scope of the plan and act for the exclusive benefit of plan participants and beneficiaries, rather than for their own or another party's gain.

[6] We have previously reported that plan sponsors may still pay some plan recordkeeping fees but participants bear them in a growing number of plans. GAO, *Private Pensions: Changes Needed to Provide 401(k) Plan Participants and the Department of Labor Better Information on Fees*, GAO-07-21 (Washington, D.C.: Nov.16, 2006).

Figure 1: Structure of Service Provider Arrangements in 401(k) Plans

Plan participant
Makes contributions and allocates them according to options available within the plan

Plan sponsor
Establishes and maintains 401(k) plan; may make matching contributions

401(k) plan

Some 401(k) plans delegate much of the fund's daily operation to a bundled plan service provider

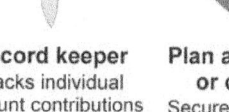

Record keeper
Tracks individual account contributions and returns

Plan asset trustee or custodian
Secures 401(k) plan's assets in a bank

Fund manager
Manages the assets of investment funds selected by participant

Other participant customer services
Provides telephone or web-based service to participants

Investment advisor
Assists with selecting investment options for the plan

Bundled plan service provider
Directly employs or contracts with an array of service providers to offer a number of services

Source: GAO analysis of information from industry practitioners.

Note: Services can be bundled or unbundled with investment management services or advisory services. Under a bundled service arrangement, the plan sponsor hires a company that provides multiple services directly or through subcontracts. Under unbundled arrangements, the sponsor uses a combination of service providers.

401(k) service providers are typically overseen by various U.S. federal and state regulators. Labor's Employee Benefits Security Administration (EBSA) has numerous responsibilities related to the oversight of 401(k) plans and protection of 401(k) participants' assets,[7] including educating and assisting plan sponsors and participants, investigating alleged violations of ERISA, responding to requests for interpretations of ERISA through advisory opinions and rulings, and making determinations to exempt transactions that would otherwise be prohibited under ERISA. However, as we have previously reported, Labor's civil enforcement efforts for plan service providers are largely limited by the extent to which the provider functions as a fiduciary under ERISA,[8] and many providers are reported to commonly structure their relationships with sponsors in a manner that avoids being subject to these fiduciary standards.[9] To carry out its enforcement duties, Labor has offered voluntary compliance programs and has relied primarily on leads from participants, plan sponsors, and other agencies to conduct targeted investigations on specific types of plans and service providers.[10] In addition to Labor's role, the specific investment products commonly offered in 401(k) plans fall under the authority of the applicable securities, banking, or insurance regulators. These regulators include the Securities and Exchange Commission (SEC), federal and state banking agencies, and state insurance commissioners as follows:

- SEC, among other responsibilities, regulates securities markets and issuers, including mutual funds, under various securities laws.

- Federal agencies charged with oversight of banks—primarily the Federal Reserve Board, the Office of the Comptroller of the Currency,

---

[7]The Employee Benefits Security Administration (EBSA) also has oversight responsibilities related to other types of DC plans, as well as DB plans. The Internal Revenue Service also oversees various aspects of 401(k) contributions under the Internal Revenue Code.

[8]29 U.S.C. § 1002(21)(A). On October 22, 2010, Labor proposed a revised definition of the term "fiduciary," 75 Fed. Reg. 65,263 (2010) and, subsequently, by News Release Number: 11-1382-NAT on September 19, 2011, Labor announced it would "re-propose" its rule on the definition of fiduciary in early 2012.

[9]GAO, *401(K) Plans: Improved Regulation Could Better Protect Participants from Conflicts of Interest*, GAO-11-119 (Washington, D.C.: Jan. 28, 2011) and *Defined Benefit Pensions: Conflicts of Interest Involving High Risk or Terminated Plans Pose Enforcement Challenges*, GAO-07-703 (Washington, D.C.: June 28, 2007).

[10]GAO, *Employee Benefits Security Administration: Enforcement Improvements Made but Additional Actions Could Further Enhance Pension Plan Oversight*, GAO-07-22 (Washington, D.C.: Jan. 18, 2007).

the Federal Deposit Insurance Corporation, and state banking agencies—oversee bank investment products.

- State insurance agencies generally regulate insurance products. Some investment products may also include one or more insurance elements, which are not present in other investment options. Generally, these elements include an annuity feature and interest and expense guarantees.[11]

Labor published final regulations on October 20, 2010, to improve U.S. participant fee disclosure, as summarized in table 1.[12] These regulations require that plan sponsors provide participants core information about investments available under the plan, including performance and fee information, prior to investing and at least on an annual basis thereafter, in a chart or similar format designed to facilitate investment comparisons. Pursuant to these new regulations, participants will receive information about pertinent administrative expenses, individual expenses, and investment-related fees and expenses that they may pay throughout the year. Participants will also receive quarterly statements on plan fees and expenses deducted from their accounts along with a description of the services for which the charge or deduction was made.

---

[11]An annuity is an insurance agreement or contract that comes in a number of different forms and can (1) help individuals accumulate money for retirement through tax-deferred savings, (2) provide them with monthly income that can be guaranteed to last for as long as they live, or (3) do both. Payments from fixed annuities are generally a set regular amount, whereas payments from variable annuities may increase or decrease based on performance of the underlying investments.

[12]Fiduciary Requirements for Disclosure in Participant-Directed Individual Account Plans; Final Rule, 75 Fed. Reg. 64,910 (October 20, 2010) (codified at 29 C.F.R. § 2550.404a-5). A revised and delayed effective date for this regulation was published on July 19, 2011 (76 Fed. Reg. 42539).

Table 1: Labor's 401(k) Participant Fee Disclosure Requirements

Annual statements	*Administrative fees.* An explanation of the fees and expenses for general plan administrative services and how these fees will affect the balance of a worker's account. These fees may include legal, accounting, trustee, recordkeeping, and other administrative fees and expenses associated with maintaining the plan
	Individual fees and expenses. An explanation of any fees and expenses charged to the balance of a worker's account on an individual basis, rather than on a plan-wide basis. These fees are associated with a service or transaction that an individual may select and may include fees and expenses for plan loans, processing qualified domestic relations orders, investment advice, and brokerage windows[a]
	Investment-related fees. For each investment option in the plan, pertinent performance information, fees and expenses, and investment restrictions: • *Variable investments.* The amount (in percent and per $1,000) of fund management fees and any shareholder fees • *Fixed investments.* The fixed or stated rate of return and any shareholder fees.
	Statement on effect of fees over time.
Quarterly statements	*Administrative fees.* Actual type and amount (in dollars) of plan administrative fees charged
	Individual fees and expenses. Actual type and amount (in dollars) of individual fees and expenses charged

Source: GAO summary of Department of Labor regulations, 75 Fed. Reg. 64,910.

[a]Brokerage windows are self-directed investment options in which participants can invest in individual stocks or mutual funds.

In addition to the United States, the U.K., Australia, Chile, and Sweden each have extensive DC pension systems. However, in drawing comparisons between countries, it is important to recognize the significant social and economic differences that exist among them and with the United States. While the economies of the U.K., Australia, Chile and Sweden can be characterized as market-based, the U.K. and Sweden generally have more extensive and generous social welfare provisions than that of the United States.[13] As shown in figure 2, the size of each country's economy is far smaller than that of the United States as measured by gross domestic product (GDP). The standard of living, as measured by GDP per capita, ranges from $15,040 in Chile to $46,860 in

---

[13]While the Organisation for Economic Co-operation and Development (OECD) recently acknowledged Chile's efforts to develop its market-based economy, it generally is understood to have more moderate social welfare policies than the United States. and publicly spends less on social welfare as a percentage of its GDP. Australia is also generally considered a market-based economy, but is understood to offer similar social welfare provisions to that of the U.S. and publicly spends about the same on social welfare as a percentage of its GDP.

the United States.[14] In addition, pension assets as a share of GDP varies from 73 percent in Chile to 239.8 percent in Sweden, and DC assets as a share of total pension assets from 5.6 percent in Sweden to 100 percent in Chile.

Figure 2: Economic Data for the United States, Australia, Chile, Sweden, and the United Kingdom, 2010[a]

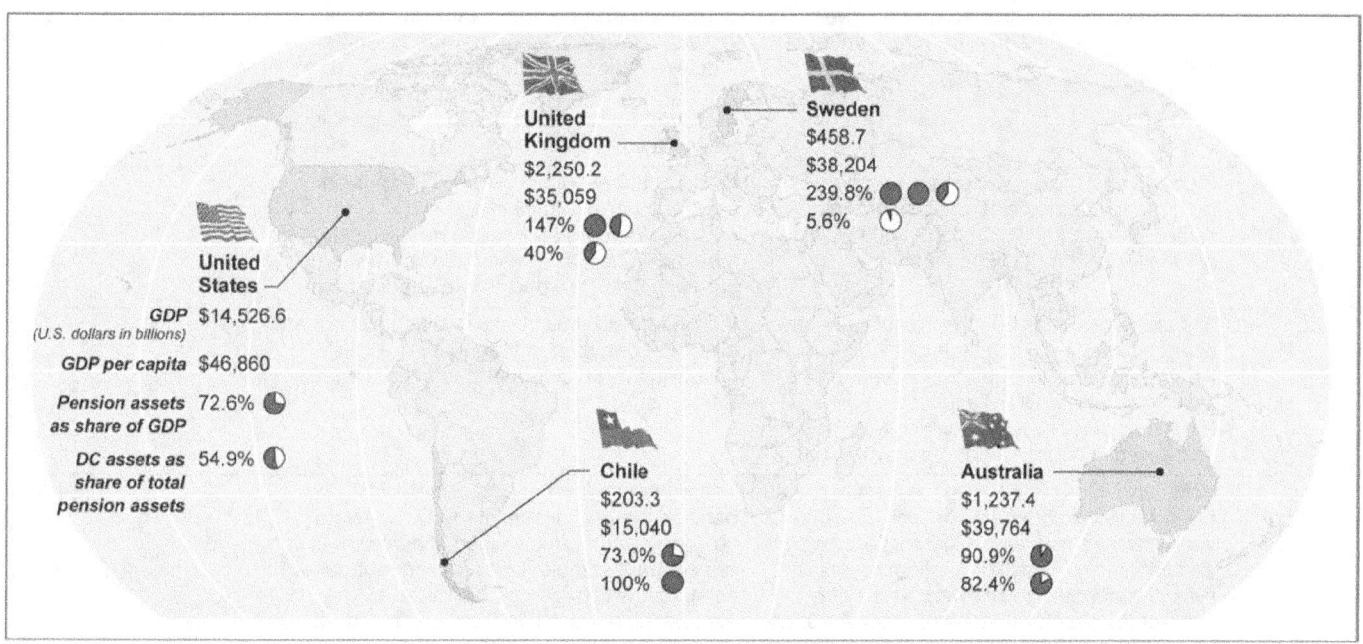

Source: IMF World Economic Outlook Database September 2011, and OECD StatExtracts, Funded Pension Indicators (statistics) extracted on October 23, 2011, government agency officials in foreign countries; Art Explosion (flags); National Atlas (base map)

[a]Total population estimates for these countries in 2011: Australia: 21.8 million, Chile: 16.9 million, United Kingdom: 62.7 million, United States: 313.2 million, Sweden: 9.1 million (see CIA World Factbook).

In addition, each country's DC system is slightly different based on their different economic and political conditions. Table 2 has key features of each country's DC system.

---

[14]GDP per capita is based on purchasing power parity, which equalizes the purchasing power of different currencies in their home countries by taking into account the relative cost of living and the inflation rates of different countries, rather than just a nominal GDP comparison.

GAO-12-328 Defined Contribution Plans

Table 2: Key Features of Case Study Countries' DC Systems

Dollars in billions USD

Country	Description of DC system	Types of plan(s)	Approximate total DC assets in 2010
Australia	Australian employers have been required to make a minimum contribution to a pension account based on a percent of employees' salaries, since 1992. The current requirement is 9 percent.	Plans in Australia are generally set up as trusts. There are three types of trust-based private pension plans available in the Australian market: industry-wide or single-employer plans with nonprofit trustees; retail plans with for-profit trustees; and self-managed accounts, where the individual is his/her own trustee.	$853
Chile	Since 1981, Chilean workers have been required to contribute 10 percent of their salary, plus an additional contribution to cover certain fees, to a DC pension plan.	Workers choose among for-profit pension service providers known as AFPs (*Administradoras de Fondos de Pensiones*) for their individual DC pension plans. There are currently 6 AFPs workers can choose from.	$148
Sweden	All Swedish workers and their employers have been required to contribute a total of 2.5 percent of the covered portion of workers' salaries to individual DC accounts in the Premium Pension System, which was introduced in pension reform passed in 1998.[a]	Individual accounts in the Swedish system are all part of one plan managed by a government-run clearinghouse, the Swedish Pensions Agency.	$62
United Kingdom	Voluntary DC plans make up most of the private pension system in the U.K. An individual may be a member of a number of different pension plans simultaneously. Since 2001, all employers with five or more workers, who were not already sponsoring a pension plan, have been required to designate a stakeholder pension provider and offer it to their workers.[b] From 2012 to 2017, all employers will be required to automatically enroll eligible employees into a pension plan and provide a minimum contribution. Employers who do not offer a qualifying pension plan will be able to auto-enroll their employees into a new national DC pension option, called the National Employment Savings Trust (NEST).[c]	There are two fundamental types of DC pension plans available in the U.K. private pension system: trust-based schemes, which are set up by employers, and contract-based schemes, which may be facilitated by the employer but are owned entirely by the individual.	$1,320

Source: GAO analysis of foreign documentation and interviews with industry experts

[a]An additional 16 percent of the covered portion of workers' salaries are contributed to notional, or non-financial, DC plans, which are designed to mimic DC plans where the pension depends on contributions and investment returns. However, in these notional accounts, the return that contributions earn is a notional one determined by average earnings growth and adjusted as necessary, not the product of investment returns in the markets. Moreover, notional DC plans are basically pay-as-you-go financed (i.e. current contributions pay for current benefits). However, Sweden also currently has a substantial buffer fund, holding assets equivalent to 25 percent of GDP, which the regulator projects will co-finance benefits beyond 2040.

[b]Stakeholder pensions are a type of low-cost personal pension with limits on the charges that providers can impose.

[c]The pensions regulator noted that a number of new trust-based plans not associated with particular employers have been launched to compete with NEST in the new auto-enrollment market.

Risk-Based Oversight Helps Some Countries' Regulatory Agencies Monitor Service Providers and Could Inform Labor as It Improves Its Oversight Approach

Service Providers' Role and Oversight

As in the U.S. DC system, service providers in the countries we reviewed play an important role and perform a range of administrative and investment management functions. The structure and role of service providers in each country's DC system varies, as described in table 3. For example, in Australia and the U.K., DC plans can be offered through different arrangements and the role of service providers varies accordingly. In some cases, the plan is run by a nonprofit entity managed by a board of trustees with representation from both employers and workers. In other cases, the plan is managed by a for-profit financial service provider with the employer playing little or no role. To address potential conflicts of interest, financial industry representatives in Australia told us that these plans, known as retail plans, have licensed trustees who are legally obliged to act in the best interests of participants, such as by reviewing the use of internal service providers. Agency officials said they look for documentation of this review of the use of service providers.

Table 3: Key roles of DC Service Providers by Country

	Key roles of DC service providers	Recordkeeping services	Investment management services	Trustee or trustee-like services
Australia	In general, trustees of Australian plans have authority to hire service providers, but the service providers' roles vary based on the type of plan:			
	Industry-wide and single-employer plans: nonprofit entities managed by a board of trustees that typically hire separate service providers for recordkeeping and investment management services.	√	√	
	Retail plans: an employee deals directly with a for-profit service provider which performs recordkeeping, investment management, and trustee services.[a]	√	√	√
	Self-managed plans: set-up by employees and entail establishing a trust and a bank account. The trust is required to be audited by a third party. Up to four people can be in the trust. The employees are the trustees and can select their investment options. The employees may hire a financial adviser or other experts to select investment options.	√	√	
Chile	In Chile, service providers play a key role in running the DC plans. For-profit pension service providers known as AFPs (*Administradoras de Fondos de Pensiones*) directly manage participants' individual accounts and provide both recordkeeping and investment management services. Each AFP offers five different investment funds with varying risk levels subject to specific regulations. AFPs hire external fund managers to provide some of these investment options.	√	√	
Sweden	The Swedish Pensions Agency, a government agency, contracts with service providers to perform investment management for the DC portion of the public pension system.[b] Nearly 800 investment options are available for participants to choose from.		√	
United Kingdom	In the U.K., the key roles of service providers vary based on the type of plan:			
	Trust-based plans: nonprofit entities typically hire one or more service providers for recordkeeping and investment management services. The plan trustees are responsible for selecting and vetting the investment options. NEST, a new nationally available plan, operates in this way.	√	√	
	Contract-based plans: an employee deals directly with a for-profit service provider which may perform both recordkeeping and investment management services. The service provider, in conjunction with an advisor or employer if necessary, selects which investment options are available to the participant.	√	√	√

Source: GAO analysis of foreign agency documentation and interviews with industry experts.

[a]According to agency officials, service providers for retail plans are often part of a conglomerate where related companies provide services for the plan.

[b]The DC portion of the public pension system is known as the Premium Pension.

In each of the countries we examined, some of the service providers are large U.S.-based companies. For example, in Australia and the U.K., representatives of U.S. service providers we spoke with said they perform a variety of functions ranging from consulting services to managing the plan, including both administrative and investment management functions. In contrast, because of the structure of the DC systems in Chile and Sweden, U.S. service providers play a more limited role and generally provide fund management or other consulting services.

While the role of service providers varies, in most of the countries we reviewed DC plans and service providers are overseen by multiple agencies—primarily a pensions regulator and a securities regulator, as described below. Moreover, in Australia and the U.K., where DC plans can be offered through different arrangements, the oversight structure differs based on the type of plan.

- In Australia, for industry-wide, single-employer and retail pension plans—called superannuation plans—the pensions regulator licenses trustees and oversees their management of the plan, including the use of service providers. Self-managed superannuation plans, on the other hand, are primarily overseen by the tax authority. In conjunction with both of these agencies, the Australian securities regulator oversees financial services, including the disclosure of fees for superannuation plans.

- In the U.K., the pensions regulator oversees trust-based plans and their use of service providers, while the securities regulator oversees the investment funds offered in these plans—particularly disclosures—and acts as the primary regulator for individual contract-based plans.[15] For other contract-based plans designated by employers but administered by for-profit service providers, oversight is jointly conducted by both the pensions regulator and the securities regulator.

- In Chile, the pensions regulator intensively oversees plan providers, including issuing licenses for them to participate in the system. On an ongoing basis, the pensions regulator monitors plan providers for compliance with investment option guidelines, reserve requirements, fee structure, and other requirements. The Chilean Ministry of Finance

---

[15]Plans must also register with the tax authority in order to obtain tax benefits.

GAO-12-328 Defined Contribution Plans

and the Central Bank coordinate with the pensions regulator on certain issues related to investment regulation.

- In Sweden, the pensions regulator administers the plan and establishes terms of participation for investment fund providers. The Swedish securities regulator, meanwhile, oversees the funds offered in the Swedish pension system, along with other investment products and services provided by the financial services industry. In addition, the securities regulator monitors the Swedish Pensions Agency as the annuity provider for the DC system.

Risk-Based Oversight Approach

In each of the four countries we reviewed, regulators use a risk-based approach to oversee DC plans and service providers and identify practices that may harm participants. In general, risk-based oversight involves developing a structured approach to identify potential risks faced by the DC system and assessing the processes in place to address those risks.[16] For example, in Chile, agency officials evaluate key features of the DC system, such as the service providers' management of the individual accounts and the composition and role of the service providers' board of directors and investment committee. Based on this assessment, the regulatory agency decides if supervisory action is necessary and, if so, what type of action—ranging from issuing guidance to imposing sanctions or withdrawing licenses to operate as a DC plan provider—is appropriate.

Based on discussions with these countries' officials and a review of the International Organisation of Pension Supervisors (IOPS) risk-based supervision literature, using a risk-based approach allows regulatory agencies in other countries to identify potential problems before they

---

[16]Guidelines provided by the International Organisation of Pension Supervisors (IOPS) specify that risk-based pension supervision should be evaluative, data driven, and forward-looking. IOPS, *Toolkit for Risk-based Pensions Supervision: Introduction to Risk-based Pensions Supervision* (2011). According to an IOPS working paper, the main risks in DC pension systems are those that impact the accumulated pension savings of participants and therefore the amount of pension benefit participants receive in retirement. They include investment risk; high costs, such as excessive fees; operating risks, such as administrating individual accounts; and managing the transition from accumulation to decumulation. John Ashcroft and Fiona Stewart, *Managing and Supervising Risks in Defined Contribution Pension Systems,* IOPS Working Paper No. 12 (October 2010).

become widespread and take proactive measures to address them.[17] For example, in both Chile and Australia, agency officials said risk-based supervision enables the pensions regulator to implement supervisory actions proactively to ensure DC plans are operating in the best interests of participants. A review of supervisory approaches by IOPS also notes that a risk-based approach is preventative in nature and increases the likelihood that significant problems will be identified and addressed at an early stage. For example, in the U.K., as part of their risk-based approach agency officials said they conduct an annual survey of plan trustees to help identify potential problems which could include high fees or conflicts of interest.[18] In addition, in Australia, the pensions regulator's approach is forward-looking in that it actively monitors and assesses the performance and situation of DC plans on an ongoing basis and then estimates the plans' capacities to manage risk.[19] Based on this assessment, the pensions regulator determines what actions need to be taken, such as more frequent and detailed data collection or working with the plan to restructure their operations or merge with another plan.[20]

In addition, agency officials and a review of supervisory approaches by IOPS cite a number of other beneficial effects of using a risk-based approach. For example, using a risk-based approach, regulators can take the following actions:

- *Allocate scarce resources more efficiently to target key risks.* By prioritizing risks, the agency can determine which DC plans or service providers require more attention and spend minimal effort on issues that pose the least threat or likely have little impact. For example, in

---

[17]IOPS is an independent international body with 70 members and observers representing about 60 countries and territories. Its purpose is, among other things, to serve as the standard-setting body on pension supervision and regulation; to promote international cooperation; to provide a worldwide forum for policy dialogue and exchange of information on pension supervision; and to participate in the work of relevant international bodies in the area of pensions.

[18]According to Labor, the Paperwork Reduction Act inhibits EBSA's ability to similarly collect information.

[19]In October 2002, the Australian pensions regulator first introduced risk assessment and supervisory response tools that formed the centerpiece of its risk-based approach.

[20]When the Australian pensions regulator identifies a superannuation plan that it considers too small, it initiates conversations with the plan trustees suggesting merger opportunities. Such mergers are eligible for tax relief.

Australia, the need for the pensions regulator to monitor a relatively large number of institutions may make compliance-based supervision either too costly or ineffective. As a result, the pensions regulator focuses on identifying higher-risk institutions that require more intensive oversight. Likewise, officials from the securities regulator in Sweden said the main advantage of risk-based supervision is the more efficient use of resources. Specifically, these officials told us that the Swedish securities regulator would not be able to conduct in-depth reviews of every fund management service provider every year; instead, the official believed that investigating only those potentially problematic service providers, as indicated by the data the regulator collects, better utilized its limited resources. In addition, the U.K. established a new risk-based pensions regulator in 2005 after a review of the previous regulator revealed inefficiencies with the compliance-based approach. In particular, the review found that numerous low-risk cases typically overwhelmed the high-risk, high-profile cases.

- *Adapt to the changing nature and complexity of financial risks.* By evaluating potential risks on an ongoing basis, a risk-based approach provides regulators flexibility to adapt to the continuing evolution of financial investment options. For example, in Chile, the pensions regulator introduced a risk-based approach to adapt to the increasing complexity of the financial markets.[21] Chile has gradually been relaxing investment regulation and, at the same time, strengthening the governance of plan providers by ensuring sound risk management practices and internal controls. Such practices include requiring plan providers to develop an investment policy and establish committees to monitor and address investments and conflicts of interest. Furthermore, in Australia, in addition to ongoing oversight of DC plans, the pensions regulator conducts ad hoc studies to address new and emerging trends, such as a study prompted by the financial crisis to increase their monitoring of the liquidity of DC investment funds.

- *Encourage pension plans to have sound risk management practices.* By assessing the processes in place for the plan to manage key risks, the regulator provides an incentive for plans to adopt good practices to improve their risk rating. For example, in its supervision of the superannuation industry, the Australian pensions regulator's main

---

[21]The adoption of a risk-based approach in Chile followed an initial assessment by the World Bank and The Financial Sector Assessment Program. It was also recommended by the OECD during Chile's accession to the organization.

GAO-12-328 Defined Contribution Plans

priority during 2010 and 2011 was to encourage more robust governance and risk management practices. To do so, it has been strengthening the capacity of some of its analysts and utilizing industry-wide analysis techniques to advise plans about the particular aspects of risk management for which they may lag behind their peers, which the regulator has found to be helpful in focusing the plans on areas where improvement is needed.

- *Promote trust and confidence in the regulator's role.* Establishing a systematic and consistent approach enhances confidence in the regulator's methods and in the pension system in general. For example, the Australian pensions regulator's use of a structured framework for risk assessment in pension plans in its risk-based approach is reported to have improved the consistency of its oversight outcomes by allowing for more standardized reactions to supervisory issues across a large number of service providers and supervisors, which enhances the pension industry's confidence in the regulator's methods and procedures.

Table 4 below summarizes the main differences between risk-based and compliance-based approaches.

Table 4: Main Features of Alternate Regulatory Approaches

Risk-based	Compliance-based
Regulators • identify potential risks, • assess mitigating factors and proper management of all risks, and • target scarce supervisory resources at supervised entities deemed as most at risk	Regulators • focus on breach of laws, rules, and regulations, and • give the same degree of attention to all funds
Approach is preventative, forward-looking, flexible	Approach focuses on a given point in time, often relies on complaints
Supervised pension plans or service providers have an incentive to strengthen risk management	Supervised pension plans or service providers focus on compliance with rules rather than risk management
Regulators can benchmark supervised entities and assess overall industry	It is difficult for regulators to get meaningful comparisons across supervised entities

Source: GAO summary of International Organisation of Pension Supervisors documentation.

IOPS notes that the introduction of risk-based supervision should be viewed as a movement along a continuum from one extreme of complete reliance on a compliance-based system to one where the emphasis of supervision is a function of risk, as described in the text box below. In addition, according to IOPS, regulators in many countries have been or are planning to utilize risk-based supervisory approaches, but implementation varies. For example, the Chilean pensions regulator has maintained some compliance procedures around quantitative investment limits in addition to its assessments of AFPs' (*Administradoras de Fondos de Pensiones*) investment risks. Thus, a risk-based approach may contain compliance-based elements. IOPS also notes that the regulator's active communication with the pension community can help it overcome the challenges associated with moving to risk-based oversight from compliance-based oversight.[22]

Moving from Risk-Based to Compliance-Based Supervision

International Organisation of Pension Supervisors (IOPS) guidance to pensions supervisors in its Toolkit for Risk-Based Pensions Supervision, includes a discussion about the interaction and complementary nature of risk-based and compliance-based supervision. According to IOPS,

> [m]oving towards RBS [risk-based supervision] is often accompanied by the deregulation of strict rules and a move towards a more 'prudential' approach to regulation, applying more high level principles. Yet RBS can be applied whether a rules-based or a principles-based form of regulation is in place. There is no one, perfectly deregulated model which all countries should be striving towards. Some pension systems (e.g. mandatory systems) requiring greater levels of protection are likely to apply more comprehensive rules than others. Whether risk is controlled via rules or via prudential regulations simply changes the nature and focus of the supervisory approach. Likewise, there is no need for an either/or choice between RBS and a more traditional or rules-based supervisory approach (i.e. simply checking for compliance with regulations). RBS does not mean having no rules or compliance procedures in place... Both methods can and should be blended according to the nature of the pension system which is being overseen. The key is to find the mix which is most appropriate according to the nature of the pension system, the capacity of the supervisory authority, and the level of development of the pension industry

Source: IOPS Toolkit for Risk-based Pensions Supervision, Module 0.

---

[22]Active communication could include issuing guidance to regulated pension plans explaining requirements and good practices, ensuring that communication with regulated pension plans is ongoing, and working closely with industry professionals such as accountants and actuaries, which can help regulated pension plans apply standards.

In general, risk-based oversight requires extensive data collection and analysis to identify individual risks at the entity level, as well as systemic risks that occur as a result of changes in the financial, economic, or social environment, and affect all or most of the entities in the DC system. However, the implementation of a risk-based approach varies and the regulators in the countries we reviewed adapt it to the unique features of their DC system, as described in the text box below.

Examples of Risk-Based Supervision by Other Countries' Pensions Regulators

Australia

The pensions regulator identifies main risk areas and evaluates how plans are addressing them, which include (1) board membership and management of the plan, (2) market and investment risk, and (3) operational risk (recordkeeping and management of outsourcing contracts). For each risk category, the pensions regulator scores plans from low (zero) to high (4). For example, to assess investment risk, it evaluates whether the plan has a clear investment strategy. A plan rated as "extreme risk" would have a high concentration of assets in one product market and high exposure to volatility. For the board of the plan, the regulator's staff evaluates key factors, such as the quality, skills, and experience of all directors, whether the board meets composition and independence requirements, and potential conflicts of interest at the board level. In determining the risk ratings, the regulator's staff collects and analyzes financial data and other information on a regular basis. Superannuation plans with at least $50 million in assets are required to report quarterly performance data, in addition to the standard annual reporting. The pensions regulator uses quarterly data on returns to check for unusual trends, which may prompt further investigation. If necessary, staff also conduct on-site visits with plans and service providers.

Chile

The pensions regulator evaluates key aspects of the DC system, such as management of the plan provider, investment risk, and operational risk. The limited number of plan providers, six as of 2011, allows the regulator to closely monitor the operation and performance of each one, including risk areas specific to a plan provider. For example, the regulator collects and analyzes data from plan providers on a daily and ad hoc basis on investment holdings and other issues. Pension industry representatives said that the regulator's data collection efforts help to keep the agency knowledgeable about the system and well-positioned to act when necessary.

United Kingdom

The pensions regulator uses a standard model for risk assessment, but does not apply individual risk scores to each plan on an annual basis because of the large number of plans the agency oversees—nearly 46,000 DC plans and over 1,000 hybrid plans with some DC benefits. Instead, the regulator collects information annually from large DC plans and up to every 3 years from smaller DC plans, which inform the regulator's risk-based approach.

Source: GAO analysis of foreign agency documentation and interviews with officials and industry experts.

Note: The Swedish pensions regulator operates the Swedish Premium Pension system and has direct agreements with service providers, from which it collects information on service provider fees and transaction costs, among other things. The Swedish securities regulator takes a risk-based approach in its oversight of Swedish funds that can be included in the Premium Pension system.

GAO-12-328 Defined Contribution Plans

Labor's Oversight Approach: Risk-Based versus Compliance-Based

In contrast to the other countries we reviewed, in the United States, Labor has not yet targeted enforcement efforts based on broad, ongoing risk assessments, or assessments of key areas of noncompliance with ERISA. Rather than using a risk-based approach, Labor has primarily relied on reports or complaints obtained from participants, plan sponsors, the media, and other agencies to conduct targeted investigations on specific topics. As we reported in 2007 and 2011, this approach generally limits Labor to leads identified by these sources and not those potential violations that may be more complex or hidden in nature.[23]

To address these limitations, in 2011 Labor officials told us that they have taken preliminary actions to develop a more risk-based approach to enforcement. For example, agency officials said Labor has adopted the following measures:

- Labor has begun implementing routine compliance examinations. These examinations will allow Labor to assess the effectiveness of its current enforcement efforts and allow better targeting of its limited resources.

- To address risk assessment trends, Labor has established a National Enforcement Library to serve as a "knowledge management" tool for the agency, which will provide information on current trends and emerging developments in plan investment and management.

While Labor is taking preliminary steps to improve its oversight, the more extensive risk-based approaches taken by the countries we reviewed allow them to take preventative measures and address the shortcomings of relying only on complaints. For example, the Chilean pension regulator started introducing a risk-based approach in 2006 to adapt to the increasing complexity of financial markets given that it is not feasible to monitor all the operations of financial institutions. Agency officials said that adopting a risk-based approach allows them to take action that is preventative in nature. Furthermore, in the U.K., officials from the pensions regulator said that they rely, in part, on participant complaints

---

[23]GAO-07-22 and GAO-11-119. In addition, Labor's enforcement efforts regarding potential conflicts of interest related to investment advice have not addressed potential violations by non-ERISA fiduciary service providers. This applies to Labor's civil investigations. However, according to Labor, for its criminal investigations the subject need not be an ERISA fiduciary because an allegation of fraud is sufficient to trigger Labor's jurisdiction.

and whistle-blowing to identify problems, but this is not effective with DC plans because of the asymmetry in information between service providers and participants. In general, officials said that participants tend to be disengaged and, even if they review disclosures, many lack the knowledge to understand the information provided to them. As a result, officials said that participants do not understand enough about their plans to identify potential problems. By adopting a risk-based approach instead, the pensions regulator, in its view, has been able to identify the greatest risks and work with plans to resolve issues.[24]

Fee Disclosure Strategies Improved Transparency in Some Countries, and Similar Strategies Could Benefit U.S. Participants

Fee Disclosure Formats

Some other countries with well-developed DC systems, including Chile, Sweden, and Australia, have taken steps to make fee disclosures simpler and more comparable, requiring that disclosures to participants be presented in consistent, summary formats. Officials in each of these countries told us that improved fee disclosures provide their participants transparency about the fees they are paying for their DC plans, which may help participants make informed decisions about their investments.[25]

---

[24]The U.K. pensions regulator is currently in the process of developing a new regulatory framework for DC plans which will be based on a segmented approach (e.g., larger plans tend to be better run and achieve economies of scale, whereas smaller plans are more likely to have lower governance standards and higher charges).

[25]These officials also noted that the enhanced disclosures may not capture all fees, like transaction costs, and government and industry surveys have shown that some participants do not read the disclosures. Swedish Pensions Agency, *Surveys About The Orange Envelope of 2011* (Stockholm, Sweden: April 2011). Social Protection Surveys have been conducted in Chile since 2002 and the last available year is 2009. In addition, the Chilean pensions regulator conducts focus groups.

Consistent with the approaches taken by these countries, research based on behavioral economics indicates that useful disclosure approaches include standardizing the types of fees and the formats in which they are presented in order to facilitate comparisons across different investment options.[26] For example, Chile, Sweden, and Australia reported making the following changes to their fee disclosures to increase transparency from previous disclosures:

- To increase awareness of fees among Chilean workers, the Chilean pensions regulator requires that statements sent to participants every 4 months use more understandable vocabulary and provide a summary of fees paid in the participant's statement. The summary includes graphics and a table with a comparison of fees across plans, as well as a personal pension projection (which translates the current account balance into an estimated total benefit amount received at retirement given certain assumptions). Fees included in the participant statements are expressed as a percentage and in Chilean pesos and reflect all administration fees and some fund management fees that a participant may pay.[27]

- In Sweden, the Swedish Pensions Agency sends fee information to all Premium Pension participants as part of an annual, individualized participant statement. This includes the total administration and fund management fee that participants paid and summary information on fund management fees for each fund a participant is invested in that allow comparison among the options chosen.[28] Funds are required to report their fees to the Swedish Pensions Agency, and the Swedish Pensions Agency consolidates it in a standard format for participants. In addition, the Swedish Pensions Agency publishes fund management fees for all investment options in the system on its

---

[26]John A. Turner and Hazel A. Witte, *Fee Disclosure to Pension Participants: Establishing Minimum Requirements*, International Centre for Pension Management Sponsored Research, Joseph L. Rotman School of Management, University of Toronto (Toronto, Canada: August 2008).

[27]Fees for external fund management that are deducted from the external funds to determine the fund's performance are not included in this total, but the Chilean pensions regulator requires plan providers to report these fees to the regulator and publishes this information online on a regular basis.

[28]Because the Swedish Pensions Agency charges one administrative charge for all participants, the fund management fee is the pertinent fee for comparison purposes.

website, which further allows individuals the opportunity to compare investment fund fees. A Swedish official noted that transparency is higher now than it was 10 years ago and that awareness of the importance of fees seems to have increased among participants and the media.

- The Australian government has made improvements to its participant disclosures. Participants receive a Product Disclosure Statement when they first join an Australian superannuation plan and periodic statements at least annually thereafter that itemize fund earnings and how much has been taken out of a participant's account in aggregate administrative and investment management fees.[29] As described in table 5, 2005 regulations have enhanced and streamlined the fee disclosures that participants receive and provide greater certainty and consistency by defining the fees and costs that were included in a standardized fees and costs template. Officials noted that these improved disclosures have increased the transparency and comparability of data and felt that participants were more aware of cost issues with respect to their superannuation plans. For example, Australian officials said that the purpose of requiring the "example of annual fees and costs table" in participant disclosures is to create a more easily comparable format for fees across different service providers.

---

[29]Self-managed superannuation funds require a lower level of disclosure, but are still subject to some of the same disclosure requirements as other superannuation plans.

Table 5: Australia's Fee Disclosure Requirements

Product Disclosure Statements (provided before consumer purchases product)	**Fees and costs template**	A standardized fee template that simplifies the disclosure of fees and costs and allows for more effective comparison across products. This template includes information about the amount of a fee or cost, how the fee or cost is charged, the frequency of the payment, its timing, and whether it is negotiable.
	Additional explanation of fees and costs section	A separate section that includes additional important information about fees and costs, such as adviser compensation, transactional and operational costs, how to negotiate lower fees, and details about any fee changes. This information is kept separate in order to preserve the simplicity of the fees and costs template.
	Example of annual fees and costs table	Provides an illustrative example of fees and charges in a balanced investment option[a] for a typical account balance and level of contributions (e.g., AUD 50,000 account balance and an annual contribution of AUD 5,000).
	Consumer advisory warning box	Emphasizes to consumers the importance of considering the benefit they will receive from the services they will pay for. It also shows the compounding value of fees and costs and how a small difference in a fund's investment performance or fees can have a significant effect on long-term investment returns.
	Shorter Product Disclosure Statement requirements[b]	Maximum 8-page Product Disclosure Statement with prescribed minimum font size and section headings so consumers can easily find important information in the Product Disclosure Statement and compare across products.
Periodic statements (ongoing disclosures provided at least annually)	**Other management costs**	An item that shows the approximate amount, stated in Australian dollars, of management costs that were not paid directly out of a worker's account but may have affected their investments. This may include costs of investing through a trust or other structure that holds underlying investment assets, which ensures that layers of management costs are captured when there is a chain of entities involved.
	Total fees paid by participant	An item that shows a single dollar amount—in Australian dollars—that includes the total fees a member or product holder paid during the period. This amount does not include transactional and operational costs that may have been incurred.

Source: GAO summary of foreign agency documentation.

[a]A balanced investment option is defined as the investment option in the plan with an asset mix of 70 percent higher-risk investments and 30 percent lower-risk investments, or the investment option in the plan that is as close as practicable to this asset mix. This option was considered to be the most appropriate for comparison purposes across plans. If the plan does not offer a balanced investment option, the example table is to be based on the plan's default investment option. If the plan offers neither, the example should be based on the investment option with the most funds invested.

[b]These requirements for superannuation plans are still being implemented. According to the Australian Securities and Investments Commission, all new plans and certain existing plans had to comply as of June 22, 2011, but all other Product Disclosure Statements have to comply by June 22, 2012.

As described in table 5, Australian Product Disclosure Statements are required to include a "consumer advisory warning box" which encourages consumers to shop around and contains an example that displays the effect of fees and expenses on a participant's account. This example, depicted in figure 3, shows the actual impact of fees over time in Australian dollar amounts, demonstrating to participants why they should pay attention to even small differences in fees.

Figure 3: Consumer Advisory Warning Box in Australian Product Disclosure Statement

> **DID YOU KNOW?**
>
> Small differences in both investment performance and fees and costs can have a substantial impact on your long term returns.
>
> ---
> For example, total annual fees and costs of 2% of your fund balance rather than 1% could reduce your final return by up to 20% over a 30 year period (for example, reduce it from $100 000 to $80 000).
> ---
>
> You should consider whether features such as superior investment performance or the provision of better member services justify higher fees and costs.
>
> You may be able to negotiate to pay lower contribution fees and management costs where applicable. Ask the fund or your financial adviser.
>
> **TO FIND OUT MORE**
>
> If you would like to find out more, or see the impact of the fees based on your own circumstances, the **Australian Securities and Investments Commission (ASIC)** website (www.fido.asic.gov.au) has a *[superannuation or managed investment fee]* calculator to help you check out different fee options.

Source: Mercer Legal Pty Ltd.

Note: Example provided by Mercer Legal Pty Ltd. According to Mercer representatives, the example includes prescribed wording and format required by Australian law (regulations made under the Corporations Act 2001) for superannuation product disclosure as of November 2011. Bolded box added for emphasis.

Personalized Fee Information

Some countries require that participants receive personalized information about the total amount they pay in fees over a given time period and a comparison of that personalized information to a benchmark (lowest-cost fee or fee paid by the average participant) for additional context. For example, in Sweden, as shown in figure 4, the participant statement sent annually includes standard information on administrative and fund management fees paid for each fund.[30] The "fund fee percent" is presented for each fund the participant invested in, and an "average pension saver" fund fee percent is provided for comparison. In addition, the total amount subtracted for administrative and fund fees from the participant's account balance for the year is disclosed.

---

[30]Transaction fees, however, are directly deducted from the fund returns and reported in aggregate in the Swedish Pensions Agency's annual report.

Figure 4: Example of Sweden's Fee Disclosure Requirements for Premium Pension Participants

Your pension accounts

Your savings towards the national public pension during 2010.

Changes in 2010 in SEK	Income pension	Premium pension
Value 2009-12-31	823 514	70 761
Pension credit for 2009	50 480	7 887
From deceased contributors	582	54
Administration and fund fees	- 383	- 330
Change in value	-23 885	8 258 *
Value 2010-12-31	850 308	86 630

*539 SEK is included here as interest on pension credit for 2009.

To date you have saved this much towards your national public pension   **936 938 SEK**

Your premium pension

In the table you can see the development of your premium pension during 2010 and the fees that you pay for fund management. You can compare this with the information for the average pension saver. New premium pension credits are invested according to the breakdown of your latest choice.

Premium Pension Account 2010-12-31	Value SEK	Change in value per cent	Fund fee per cent	*Chosen allocation per cent	Current allocation per cent
Equity Fund Sverige	29 895	18	0,19	30	35
Equity Fund Global	22 286	14	0,35	25	26
Interest Fund Sverige	7 087	2	0,14	10	8
Generation Fund	20 812	11	0,19	25	24
Medical Products Fund	6 550	1	0,50	10	7
Total	86 630	13	0,26	100	100
The average pension saver		12	0,32		

Keep in mind that high fees can entail a less change in value for you as a saver

Source: Swedish Pensions Agency.

Note: These excerpts from an example of an annual Swedish participant statement simply and clearly show the total amount—in Swedish kronor—that the participant paid in fees. In addition, the disclosure document also shows the participant's fee detail for the specific funds in which a participant has chosen to invest their Premium Pension contributions, by fund and in total, and provides the total fund fee as a percent for the average pension saver for comparison purposes. Bolded boxes added for emphasis.

In Chile, participants not only receive personalized fee disclosures, but they also receive information about what the participant would have been charged if they belonged to the other five plans, including the lowest-cost option as shown in figure 5. Thus, the participant can see the specific difference in fees they are paying through their plan compared to the lowest-cost option.[31]

Figure 5: Example of Chile's Fee Disclosure Requirements

Personalized fee disclosure example
(Individual with a taxable income of US $760 as of November 2011)

FEE COSTS
If someone would make monthly contributions for 12 months, the total fees paid to the system would be:

A.F.P.	Total annual percentage fee		Annual difference with respect to the least costly AFP
	%	(US$)	(US$)
CAPITAL	1,44	131	27
CUPRUM	1,48	135	31
HABITAT	1,36	124	20
MODELO	1,14	104	—
PLANVITAL	2,36	215	111
PROVIDA	1,54	140	36

Source: Superintendence of Pensions, Chile.

Note: Every four months, Chilean participants receive a pension disclosure that includes a table of personalized costs, such as the one seen in this excerpt, which shows—in Chilean pesos and as a percent—the total fees they would pay in any of the plans in which they could invest their pension contributions and the annual difference between the plans' fees. For the purpose of this example, the Chilean pensions supervisor has provided the table in U.S. dollars based on the exchange rates in November 2011. Bolded box added for emphasis.

Labor's Fee Disclosure Requirements

In their current form, Labor's fee disclosure improvements will not actually show U.S. participants the effect of fees on their accounts over time. Instead, Labor's recently issued regulations will require that participant

[31]Because of the small number of plans available to Chilean participants, this type of disclosure is likely clearer than it would be if participants were offered many more choices.

disclosures include generic language on the long-term impact of fees and expenses, including that the cumulative effect of fees and expenses can reduce the growth of a participant's account, as shown in figure 6. This generic language does not include the actual effect of fees over time in dollar amounts.

Figure 6: Example of Labor's 401(k) Participant Disclosure Requirement Demonstrating the Effect of Fees

The cumulative effect of fees and expenses can substantially reduce the growth of your retirement savings. Visit the Department of Labor's Web site for an example showing the long-term effect of fees and expenses at http://www.dol.gov/ebsa/publications/401k employee.html. Fees and expenses are only one of many factors to consider when you decide to invest in an option. You may also want to think about whether an investment in a particular option, along with your other investments, will help you achieve your financial goals.

Source: U.S. Department of Labor.

Note: Labor's recently issued regulations will require that participant disclosures include generic language on the long-term impact of fees and expenses, an example of which is shown in this excerpt. This example states that the cumulative effect of fees and expenses can substantially reduce the growth of a participant's account but does not show, in dollar amounts, how a participant's account balance could differ given differing fee levels. The link to Labor's website, which is provided in this example, does show, in dollar amounts, how a participant's account balance could differ given differing fee levels, but participants do not specifically see this level of detail in their fee disclosures.

In addition, the fee disclosures U.S. participants will receive under Labor's new fee disclosure requirements do not provide participants the total amount that they have actually paid in one place, or a cumulative cost amount. Labor's new participant disclosure regulations will require that participants receive quarterly statements on some plan fees and expenses deducted from their accounts along with a description of the services for which the charge or deduction was made. However, fund management fees are not included in this quarterly requirement. For these fund management fees, as shown in figure 7, participants will receive annual disclosures that report them as a percentage and as a dollar amount (based on a $1,000 account balance), but do not specifically report the dollar amount of fees paid by a participant based on their account balance. In order to discern their total fee, participants will have to calculate the fund management fees they paid based on their account balance and the information provided in the annual disclosure, and add the fees separately disclosed in their quarterly statements to that calculated amount.

Figure 7: Example of Annual Fee Disclosure Requirements for 401(k) Participants under Labor's New Regulations

Name / Type of Option	Total Annual Operating Expenses		Shareholder-Type Fees
	As a %	Per $1000	
Equity Funds			
A Index Fund/ S&P 500	0.18%	$1.80	$20 annual service charge subtracted from investments held in this option if valued at less than $10,000.
B Fund/ Large Cap	2.45%	$24.50	2.25% deferred sales charge subtracted from amounts withdrawn within 12 months of purchase.
C Fund/ International Stock	0.79%	$7.90	5.75% sales charge subtracted from amounts invested.
D Fund/ Mid Cap ETF	0.20%	$2.00	4.25% sales charge subtracted from amounts withdrawn.

Table 3—Fees and Expenses

Source: U.S. Department of Labor.

Note: Bolded box added for emphasis.

While Labor has made recent improvements to U.S. participants' fee disclosures, fee disclosure improvements made by some of the countries we reviewed may provide more transparent disclosures. U.S. participants typically do not receive the simple, useful, and more targeted information about their DC retirement plans and investment options that is provided to participants in Chile, Sweden, and Australia, which could be why recent research shows that U.S. participants have misconceptions about the fees they pay.[32] For example the Australian consumer advisory warning box shows how a small difference in a fund's investment performance or fees can have a significant effect on long-term investment returns. (See fig. 3.) In addition, participants in Sweden and Chile received personalized fee information that shows the exact amount, in Swedish kronor and Chilean pesos, that participants paid, without any need for calculation on the part of the participant. (See figs. 4 and 5.)

---

[32]According to a February 2011 survey conducted by AARP, 71 percent of plan participants thought they paid no 401(k) fees, while only 23 percent knew they paid fees. In addition, the survey found that 62 percent were unaware of how much they paid in fees for their plan and 32 percent did not feel knowledgeable about the impact that fees could have on their retirement savings. AARP, *401(k) Participants' Awareness and Understanding of Fees* (Washington, D.C.: February 2011).

Targeted Strategies Used by Some Countries Lower Fees

The Importance of Using Direct Measures to Address Fees

While simpler, personalized disclosures increase transparency and can help participants make informed decisions about their accounts, officials and industry experts in the countries we reviewed noted that disclosure alone has not been successful at reducing fees. In particular, officials and industry experts in each country said that many participants are disengaged and do not make active decisions, even when it would lower their fees. Thus, officials in these countries told us that they have decided not only to improve participant disclosures but also to take complementary approaches to reduce fees, since fees can significantly reduce participants' account balances over time. Officials in some of the countries we reviewed emphasized the importance of taking direct measures to lower fees—research shows that a failure to ensure adequate retirement savings may increase reliance on public retirement programs, which would further increase governments' future financial burdens.

Source: GAO analysis of foreign agency documentation and interviews with officials and industry experts.

Consolidating and Streamlining Service Providers' Administrative Functions

Officials in the countries we reviewed told us they have been successful at reducing administrative and fund management fees by consolidating and streamlining administrative functions, such as account processing, recordkeeping, and participant communications.[33] Moreover, each country uses a slightly different approach to provide this efficiency. For example, Sweden and the U.K. have each consolidated administrative services into one entity, which has improved administrative efficiency by eliminating

---

[33]In comparison, the amount of fees a DC plan participant pays in the U.S. can vary considerably across plans. As we previously reported, U.S. participants tend to pay the same types of fees (e.g. investment management and recordkeeping fees), but the amount of those fees depends on a number of factors, which could be related to the employer's size and actions it takes as a plan sponsor. For example, sponsors may decrease fees by combining or pooling assets to access certain investment products or negotiate with service providers. However, U.S. workers are limited to the plans offered by their employers and some of those plans charge higher fees than others. GAO, *Retirement Savings: Better Information and Sponsor Guidance Could Improve Oversight and Reduce Fees for Participants,* GAO-09-641 (Washington, D.C.: Sept. 4, 2009).

duplicative processing functions and allowed that entity to complete bulk trades with fund providers.[34] Representatives from service providers in both countries said this structure allows them to significantly reduce their costs—and thus to lower their fees—because they only receive one aggregate transfer each day from the administrator, they do not have to maintain individual accounts, and they do not have to market to participants. As shown in figure 8, Sweden's centralized entity is a government body and it requires that providers rebate a substantial portion of their charges to participants in order to acknowledge the cost savings at the fund level of not completing those consolidated administrative activities.[35] Because of this consolidated structure, average total administration and fund management fees that the participant pays are about 0.50 percent,[36] which have been shown to be lower than the rest of the Swedish market and low by global standards.[37]

---

[34]Sweden's Premium Pension system represents the only traditional DC portion of the public DC system. The U.K.'s NEST is a nationally available plan, implemented along with the U.K.'s auto-enrollment requirements, in order to provide all employers a low-cost plan in which to enroll their employees. NEST's trustee body has a public service obligation to accept any employer who wishes to offer the plan to its employees.

[35]According to the Swedish Pensions Agency, fund providers for the Swedish system are required to rebate from about 55 to 81 percent of their retail fee based on the type of funds they offer (equity or bond) and their aggregate market share in the system. Providers send rebates to the administrative body every 3 months, although it distributes rebates to affected participants in the following year.

[36]Administrative fees in Sweden have fallen from 0.30 to 0.16 percent between 2001 and 2011. Swedish officials expect to continually lower administrative fees because the system's assets will continue to grow, and since administrative costs are typically fixed, they will decline per participant as the system's assets grow. Sweden charges fees for fund management separate from administrative fees, and these fees in January 2012 ranged from 0 to 2.57 percent.

[37]Turner and Witte (2008) and Tapia, W. and J. Yermo (2008), "Fees in Individual Account Pension Systems: A Cross-Country Comparison", *OECD Working Papers on Insurance and Private Pensions,* No. 27, OECD publishing, © OECD. doi:10.1787/236114516708.

Figure 8: The Structure of Sweden's Premium Pension System Helps Lower Administrative and Fund Management Fees

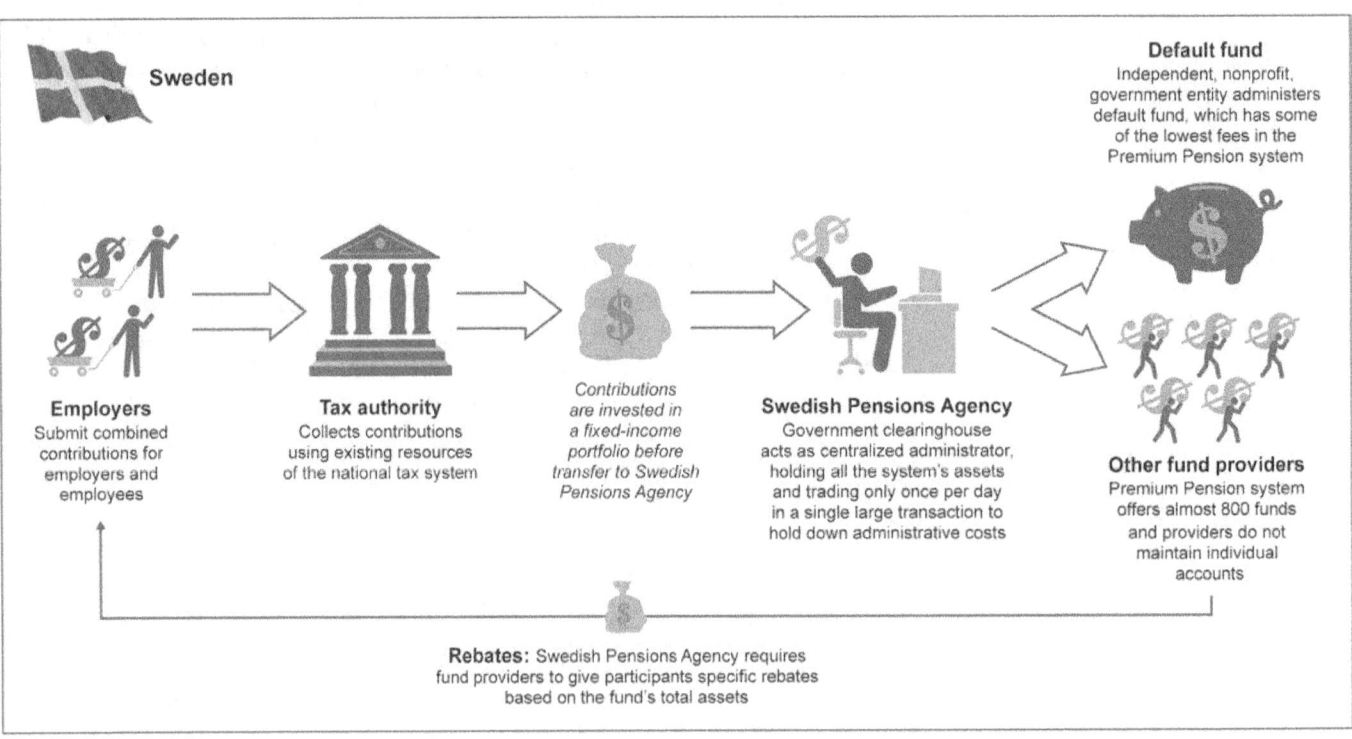

Source: GAO analysis of foreign agency documentation and interviews with industry experts.

As described in figure 9, the U.K. has also set up its nationally available, low-cost plan by consolidating administrative functions, but it has used one for-profit service provider for administration and a limited number of additional for-profit service providers for fund management.[38] U.K. plan representatives said that consolidating administrative functions has increased their scale and bargaining power, which has allowed them to attain lower fees from service providers. In addition, the U.K. plan will be highly automated and provide for many self-service functions, which they expect will lower costs. This low-cost plan is expected to particularly help low-income workers employed by small employers, and experts we spoke

---

[38]While the U.K. designed this nationally available plan to be low-cost, decisions about the plan are made by a trustee body. The original members of the body were appointed by the government. The choice of future NEST trustee members will be made by the NEST trustee body and the representative member panel will participate in the recruitment and appointment of NEST's trustee members.

to noted that they anticipate huge cost savings for those workers if their employers offer the plan. Total administrative and fund management fees for this nationally available DC plan will be 0.30 percent, which is generally lower than fees participants pay for other DC plans offered in the U.K.—which typically range from 0.40 to 2.00 percent.[39]

Figure 9: The United Kingdom Has Structured Its Nationally Available Plan to Reduce Administrative and Fund Management Fees

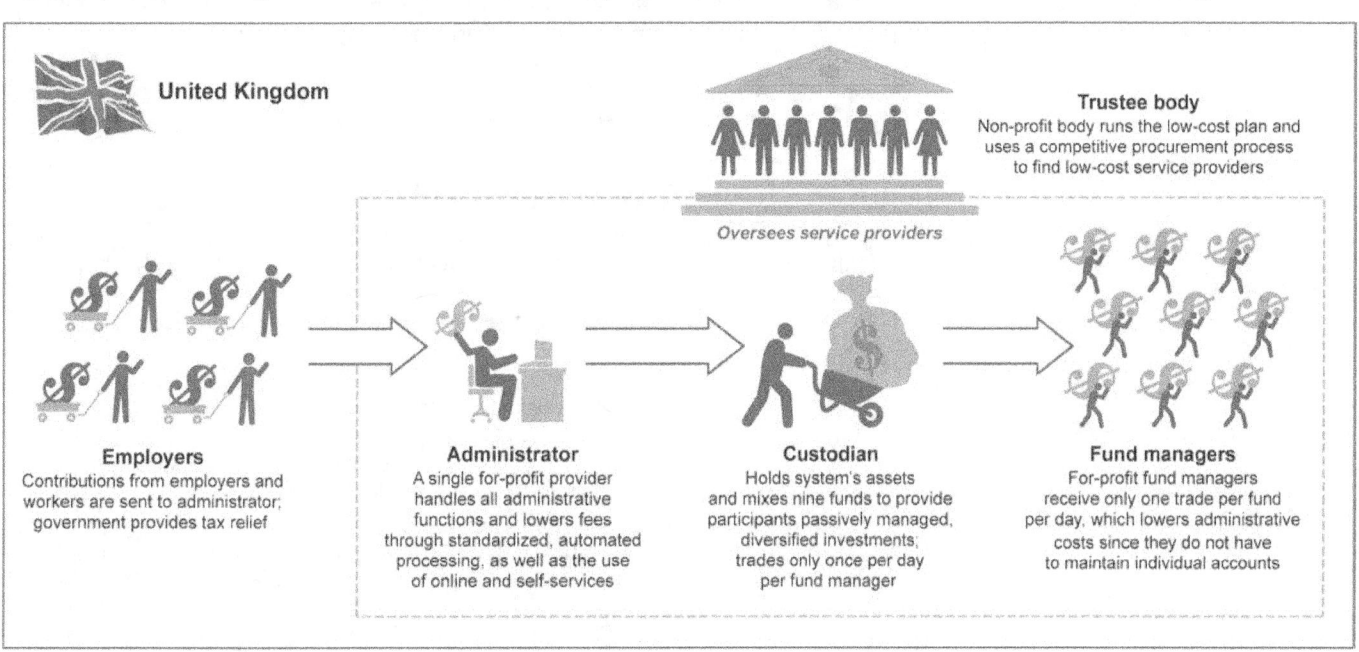

Source: GAO analysis of foreign agency documentation and interviews with industry experts.

In contrast to Sweden and the U.K.'s approach to consolidate administrative functions into one entity, the Australian pensions regulator has encouraged mergers among superannuation plans that have lowered administration fees for some participants and has also recently proposed standardized requirements to streamline administrative services within each service provider that are intended to lower fees for all participants.

---

[39]The plan also received a loan from the British government that will allow them to spread startup costs over a certain amount of time for which the plan will charge participants an additional 1.8 percent of contributions until the loan is paid off. Officials' calculations indicate that the total effective charge on participants will be about 0.50 percent per year, based on the average participant. The officials stated that they expect the loan to be repaid in about 20 years.

For example, Australia will adopt data standards to make superannuation transactions more timely and efficient, will reduce the number of accounts per member, and will make other changes, as shown in table 6. Industry experts thought that modernizing and standardizing administration, including enhanced use of technology, would effectively decrease fees in the Australian superannuation system, and a consultant estimated the new requirements would decrease fees by about 7 percent. Furthermore, industry officials estimated that the proposed requirements would save the Australian superannuation system up to AUD 1 billion annually.[40]

Table 6: Australia's Proposed Regulations to Reduce Costs through a Variety of Methods

Reform	Proposed measures
SuperStream reforms	• Implement new data and e-commerce standards for superannuation transactions to improve the quality of data in the system
	• Allow the use of tax file numbers as the primary locator of member accounts
	• Encourage the use of technology to improve processing efficiency, removing substantial manual processing
	• Improve the way plan-to-plan rollovers are processed and the way contributions are made by developing standardized forms and supporting electronic transactions
	• Help participants avoid paying unnecessary fees on multiple accounts by streamlining the process to consolidate accounts, such as through automatically consolidating any accounts with less than AUD 1,000 to the current active account unless the member opts out and allowing superannuation plans to search the Australian Taxation Office registers for any lost or unclaimed superannuation and advise the member that they may wish to consolidate their superannuation accounts
	• Enhance new employee enrollment process where employees will be able to access a listing of all their superannuation accounts from Australian Taxation Office online to assist with exercising choice
	• Establish an advisory governance body to advise on the implementation and maintenance of the standards
Securing Super reforms	• Provide better information about the amount and timing of superannuation payments to employees
	• Provide notification from plans to members on whether contributions have or have not been received

Source: GAO summary of Australian government publication.

[40] *Super System Review: Review of the Governance, Efficiency, Structure and Operation of Australia's Superannuation System* (Commonwealth of Australia, June 30, 2010).

| Default Options Are Designed to Charge Low Fees | For participants who do not actively choose where to invest their contributions, some countries have established default options that lower fees in a variety of ways, such as creating a public option default fund, increasing the use of online services, and eliminating marketing costs. For example, the Swedish government established an independent, nonprofit entity to administer the default investment fund. Officials noted that fund management fees for this fund are low compared to the other funds in the system—the equity portion charges a 0.15 percent fee and the bond portion charges a 0.09 percent fee—because it is a public option mandated by the government to be cost-effective and because it has sufficient size to command low fees from outsourced service providers.[41] A default fund official also noted that this low fee is made possible through a government subsidy for the default fund's startup costs, implemented to lessen the inequities in fees charged across generations. According to this official, 2011 is the second year in a row that the default fund generated a surplus; by 2016, the fund expects to repay the government loan and, as a result, to further decrease fees. |

Similarly, in Chile, all new entrants are defaulted to the lowest-cost plan provider for 2 years as determined by a bidding process. Most participants do not monitor or actively manage their accounts and officials noted that they tend not to switch service providers to get lower fees. The total cost for the plan provider that won the first bidding process is considerably lower than for some other providers—1.14 percent of salary[42] compared to a range of 1.36 to 2.36 percent of salary for other

---

[41]In 2010, the investment strategy for the default fund, AP7 Såfa, was updated to take a higher-risk, age-adapted approach since an increasing number of participants were choosing the default option—96 percent of new entrants in 2010, according to a default fund official—and many of those participants were young adults. AP7 Såfa also now offers different risk-level funds ("offensive," "balanced," and "cautious") that do not change based on a participant's age.

[42]The second bidding process finished in February 2012 and the AFP that won will charge 0.77 percent of salary for the 2 years starting August 2012.

GAO-12-328 Defined Contribution Plans

providers.[43] Even though costs for each plan provider differ, service providers stated that plan investment returns were very similar. Furthermore, Chilean officials reported that new participants who have no or low accumulated balances actually achieve a higher return in the low-cost plan provider than if they had chosen the provider with the best yield, which showed that these participants could save on fees without sacrificing returns. However, while the bidding process has lowered fees for new participants, it has not done so for existing participants because most have stayed with their current provider even though these providers did not lower their fees. Officials said they expect future bidding processes to lead to more competition and, thus, lower fees even further for future participants or participants who decide to switch providers.

In Australia, government officials and industry experts said recently proposed requirements for a new, simple, cost-effective default superannuation product, called MySuper, should result in considerably lower fees.[44] An industry consultant estimated that the MySuper proposals could charge around 0.66 percent of assets, which is about 30 percent less than the current industry average. In addition, MySuper default funds will have a single, diversified investment strategy and a standard set of fees. As seen in table 7, officials expect to see reduced fees since certain types of fees will be limited, but they have not explicitly

---

[43]Fee amounts are effective as of March 2012. Participants paying fees as a percent of salary pay more upfront as a percent of their account balance than participants paying asset-based fees, which have a much smoother effect over time. Fees as a percent of salary in Chile are deducted as an additional amount of a participant's salary—Chilean employers are required to remit to a Chilean plan provider (1) 10 percent of a worker's salary as a contribution and, (2) on top of that contribution, an additional percent of salary according to the provider's fee. For example, if a participant contributed to a provider that charged a 1.48 percent fee, their employer would remit 11.48 percent of their salary (10 percent contribution plus 1.48 percent fee) to the provider on the participant's behalf. While this fee represents a large portion of participants' account balances in early years, it represents less of their account balances in later years. Over a participant's lifetime, this fee could translate into an approximately 0.58 percent asset-based fee at present values.

[44]If the requirements are finalized, an Australian government release states that, from October 1, 2013, employers must make contributions for workers who have not chosen their fund, to a fund offering a MySuper product in order to satisfy superannuation guarantee obligations, and by July 1, 2017, funds will need to transfer the existing default balances of workers to a MySuper product.

capped fees.[45] All fees must be included under the standard descriptions, which officials said will allow workers, employers, and market analysts to compare funds more easily. Employers will have better information to assist with selecting a default fund and confidence that any MySuper product will meet minimum standards and offer a cost-effective superannuation plan for their workers.[46] It will also ensure that workers do not pay for any additional features or services they do not need or use. In particular, the MySuper product is restricted from including investment advice as a standard service, which an industry expert said is not widely used by participants.

---

[45]Officials note that funds will be able to offer a discounted administration fee to workers of particular employers. Funds will also have the flexibility to offer employers with more than 500 workers a MySuper product tailored to the needs of the particular workplace. To maintain transparency of these arrangements, the details of all separately tailored MySuper products and discounted administration fees will be required to be reported to the pensions regulator and will also need to be separately published by trustees.

[46]Trustees wanting to offer a MySuper product will be required to apply to the pensions regulator to be authorized for each MySuper product.

Table 7: Australia's Proposed MySuper Default Products Will Be Limited to Certain Fees

Type of fee[a]	Description	Amount allowed
Administration fee	These are fees for recordkeeping and general services required for day-to-day administration of the plan. They are typically disclosed as a fixed dollar amount, in Australian dollars.	No limitation
Investment fee (including a performance-based fee)	These fees are typically expressed as a percentage of assets and represent the cost of managing the plan's assets, including custody and indirect expenses.	Performance-based fees are subject to the following limitations:[b] • A reduced base fee that reflects the potential gains the investment manager receives from performance-based fees, taking into account any fee cap; • measurement of performance on an after-tax and after-cost basis; • an appropriate benchmark and hurdle for the asset class reflecting the risks of the actual investments; • an appropriate testing period; and • provisions for the adjustment of the performance-based fee to recoup any prior or subsequent under-performance (for example, high water marks, clawbacks, vesting arrangements, and rolling testing periods).[c]
Buy and sell spreads	Implicit when a fund buys or sells assets, the buy and sell spread is the difference between an asset's entry price and exit price and is a cost incurred by the fund each time it invests or withdraws funds.	Limited to provider's cost recovery
Exit fee	Fees charged when an individual removes his/her investments from the plan (at retirement or to move into another plan).	Limited to provider's cost recovery
Switching fee	Fees charged when the participant changes his/her investment options within the plan.	Limited to provider's cost recovery

Source: GAO analysis and summary of Australian government publication.

[a]MySuper default products are limited to these fees; MySuper providers are prohibited from charging any other fees, including hidden fees such as trailing commissions—fees paid to advisors each year the participant owns the fund so that the advisor will review the participant's holdings and provide advice. Plan trustees can charge for certain member-specific costs, such as account splitting following a family law decision.

[b]If a performance-based fee arrangement does not contain each of these provisions, the MySuper trustee must be able to justify that the differing arrangement continues to be in the best financial interests of the members of the MySuper product.

[c]High water marks provide that payment of performance fees is conditional on exceeding the maximum fund value for which the fund manager has already received performance fees. Clawbacks require recent performance fees to be paid back to plan participants if the fund suffers subsequent significant losses. Vesting arrangements lock performance fees, wholly or partially, for a period of time to align the fund manager's interests with the plan participants' interests. Rolling testing periods require that performance fees should be calculated on an ongoing basis so a longer period can be used to assess performance.

| Other Targeted Approaches | The countries we reviewed have also taken other targeted approaches which have been effective at lowering fees, such as the following: |

- *Direct regulation of types or amounts of fees.* Chile and Australia have reduced some fees participants pay by directly banning certain fees or types of fees, while the U.K. has seen certain fees decline because of explicit fee caps. Chile officials told us that they banned fees as a percent of assets and fixed fees because some participants' account balances were severely diminished after periods of little or no contributions.[47] Similarly, Australia has recently moved to restrict commission-based compensation for investment advisors because they noticed that some participants were being charged ongoing fees by advisors to plans but were not receiving ongoing advice. In the U.K., on the other hand, officials recognized that total fees could be lower for participants and implemented certain plans with explicit fee caps. According to officials we spoke to, although not many participants actually utilized these plans, their presence increased competition in the industry and substantially lowered fees.[48]

- *Direct regulation of certain service provider practices.* Australia and Sweden have moved to ban practices that have increased fees. Australia has proposed a ban on "flipping"—when a service provider rolls a participant's superannuation plan account into a personal plan, for which fees can be 2 to 3 times higher. Government officials focused on this practice because it is typically done without participants' consent. Sweden also recently banned the practice of investment advisors changing funds for their customers en-masse via computerized systems, which some advisors were doing frequently without providing individualized advice to their customers. According to Swedish representatives, this practice significantly increased transaction costs and inflated fees for some participants.

- *Increased education and licensing requirements for certain occupations.* In Australia and Chile, increased requirements for education and licensing of different industry stakeholders have

---

[47]Chile also caps fees for certain drawdown products and fees that service providers can pay to external managers for retail class shares, which have both helped to bring fees down.

[48]Officials noted that legislation requiring advisors to compare plans offered by for-profit providers to these low-cost plans with the explicit fee cap may have helped to lower fees.

decreased fees. In Australia, officials told us that increased requirements for plan trustees led to significant consolidation among certain types of plans.[49] For example, an official told us that nearly 4,000 of those plans collapsed to 400 or 500 through mergers. According to an industry expert, many of these consolidations occurred because trustees of certain superannuation plans may have decided that they had less expertise in running a superannuation plan than running their business. According to agency officials, the increased size of plans after consolidation may have led to decreased fees. In Chile, on the other hand, increased requirements for pension advisors have reduced the number of advisors and have imposed stricter rules for switching accounts among AFPs. Prior to the increased requirements, Chilean officials told us that advisors often used abusive practices to provide incentives for workers to switch accounts, such as giving workers part of the advisor's commission or other bribes and filling out the worker's form with potentially fraudulent signatures, which also caused large system costs. One service provider noted that the education and licensing requirements prohibited these practices and, thus, reduced overall costs in the system and fees for participants over time. The stricter rules for switching accounts also led to mergers and acquisitions among AFPs with less market share, which increased the size of the remaining AFPs, allowing them to charge lower fees and still remain competitive.

- *Other strategies.* The countries we reviewed have also taken other targeted approaches that have reduced fees, which are summarized in table 8, but the reduction in fees from any one of these approaches may not have been significant for all participants in the DC systems.

---

[49]Requirements of the trustee board as a whole included that they have appropriate knowledge, manage conflicts of interest, and have a policy regarding oversight of service providers.

Table 8: Other Strategies That Have Reduced Fees

Country	Strategy	Description
Chile	Participants can only invest through one plan (AFP)	The Chilean system avoids duplicative administrative costs associated with multiple accounts.
United Kingdom	Pensions Quality Mark	Introduced by the National Association of Pension Funds, an industry group of plan professionals and service providers, this voluntary mark sets a standard of excellence for employer-offered DC plans that employers can use to promote their plan. One component of the mark limits fee levels.
	Efforts to improve participant selection of annuity provider	The national Money Advice Service, which was started by the U.K. securities regulator but has since become an independent organization, publishes annuity prices on its website. It also provides information to help participants select the type of annuity best suited for them since the data shows that 2 in 3 participants select their DC plan provider for an annuity even though the cost can be up to 40 percent higher than with other providers.

Source: GAO analysis of foreign agency documentation and interviews with industry experts.

Conclusions

The countries we reviewed have taken a variety of steps to oversee service providers and improve fee disclosures. However, these nations typically did not rely primarily on improved transparency to lower fees paid by participants, but combined transparency improvements with other targeted approaches to reduce fees. Despite important social, economic, and institutional differences between the United States and these countries, the key strategies these countries used to effectively lower fees offer some potential options for the U.S. experience. Given that a number of major U.S. service providers operate in several of the countries we reviewed and have adjusted to the regulatory requirements of these strategies, similar practices could be feasible in the United States. In addition, given the size of the U.S. DC system, implementation of some of the innovative approaches to reduce fees taken by these other countries may prove to be less expensive and more efficient for U.S. service providers. As more American workers rely on DC plans for their retirement savings and since excessive fees can have an adverse effect on net savings, it is important that Labor continue to address the impact of fees on participants. Consideration of approaches used by these countries that have proven to be successful could help Labor in this effort.

Labor could learn from the positive experiences of other countries as it improves its supervisory approach and refines its participant disclosure regulations. In particular, regulatory agencies in the countries we reviewed have developed and already put into practice risk-based supervisory practices that could help Labor as it moves toward a risk-based approach in its own enforcement efforts. Given the significant role of service

GAO-12-328 Defined Contribution Plans

providers in the U.S. DC system and the complexity of fees charged for their services—including the impact of fees on participants' account balances—it is important that Labor effectively oversees plans' use of service providers. Similarly, Labor's current efforts to improve participant disclosures are a promising development, but may be strengthened by taking steps to evaluate their effectiveness, costs, and potential effect on coverage, and, as necessary, making further improvements. In this respect, the efforts taken by several countries that have improved their disclosures by making them more personalized and significantly highlighting the long-term impact of fees could prove instructive, relevant, and positive to the U.S. experience. If no action is taken to monitor and respond to potential shortcomings in participant disclosures, some participants will continue to be unaware of the fees they are paying and the long-term impact of those fees on their retirement savings.

Recommendations for Executive Action

We recommend that the Secretary of Labor take the following two actions:

- Consider other countries' experiences as Labor continues its efforts to develop a risk-based approach in supervising DC plans and their service providers, such as adopting risk-based oversight practices developed by the International Organisation of Pension Supervisors and used by the countries we reviewed that have helped them better oversee their DC plans.

- Consider recent international initiatives to improve fee transparency to assess their relevance and utility for U.S. 401(k) plan participants, such as improvements that provide summarized and personalized fee information and that show the effects of fees over time.

Agency Comments and Our Evaluation

We provided a draft of this report to the Departments of Labor, State, and the Treasury, and the Securities and Exchange Commission (SEC) for their review and comment. SEC and the Department of State did not provide comments. The Departments of the Treasury and Labor provided technical comments, which we have incorporated where appropriate. The Department of Labor (Labor) also provided written comments, which are reproduced in appendix III. Overall, Labor generally agreed with our findings and noted that it will consider our recommendations carefully as it derives insights from its own multinational pension research and policy discussions.

Regarding our recommendation on risk-based supervision, Labor agreed that other countries' experiences can sometimes be useful in evaluating U.S. policies and programs but highlighted some differences that exist among the private pension systems of the United States, Australia, Chile, Sweden, and the U.K. In general, we agree that the voluntary and heavily employer-based U.S. system has its own unique institutional and operational features—as does each other system we reviewed—and the diversity of each system makes it impossible to apply risk-based supervisory principles in a strict, uniform manner. This is why we explain that risk-based supervision can be, and has been, implemented to varying degrees along a continuum with compliance-based supervision. Specifically, Labor pointed out that the U.S. DC system is voluntary and, unlike its foreign counterparts, U.S. regulators must take account of the risk that employers will simply decline to sponsor retirement plans. We note that other countries have implemented risk-based supervision within voluntary systems and that, even in some of the more compulsory systems we reviewed, the fund provider or trustee involvement may not be required. For example, the Australian pensions regulator's risk-based approach has not driven away trustees of over 4,000 regulated superannuation plans even though it is not mandatory for those trustees to offer plans—it is only mandatory for employers to remit a portion of their employees' salaries to those plans.

Labor also noted that U.S. plans are not licensed and that Labor's foreign counterparts generally have more discretion to intervene and require actions as part of supervision of their licensed entities, whereas Labor generally must establish a violation before it can compel action. While we understand the distinction Labor makes between a regulator's authority over licensed entities versus that over nonlicensed entities, we note that Labor does have the authority to influence U.S. fiduciaries by providing guidance, publishing regulations, targeting enforcement efforts, and, if necessary, seeking legislative changes. Risk-based supervision is focused on how the regulator can better utilize its limited resources to oversee regulated entities regardless of the type of retirement savings vehicle they offer—it does not increase employers' risks. In fact, irrespective of the supervisory approach taken, regulators must decide the level of compliance complexity that the regulated entities must meet. Consequently, we believe that Labor could encourage employers to sponsor plans while balancing the complexity of compliance to avoid excessive burden. Overall, we commend Labor on starting to pursue a risk-based approach that is suitable to U.S. circumstances as part of its overall enforcement strategy—in concert with the other enforcement efforts Labor detailed in its letter.

Regarding our recommendation on fee disclosure, Labor agreed that it will look into the global experiences described in our report for possible areas of improvement as it monitors the implementation of its new regulations. Labor commended us on the excellent summary of fee transparency activities being implemented in the countries we reviewed, and noted that it is open to learning from global experiences that help drive down costs and improve retirement saving results for workers. Although Labor was impressed that regulators in the countries we reviewed tended to focus on the same issues that Labor did in its recent efforts to improve fee disclosure, it did not believe it was an appropriate time to propose changes to recent fee disclosure regulations. We continue to believe that it is important to look at what has worked well in other countries as Labor moves forward in evaluating the implementation of its new regulations. Regarding our fee disclosure findings, Labor was unclear whether the countries we reviewed had as complex of a fee structure—particularly with respect to indirect fees—as is common in the United States, whether the reported amounts for actual fees paid were precise or estimates, or what such disclosures cost. We note that there are indeed indirect fees charged in these countries, and that they are already trying to find ways to disclose to their plan participants actual fees paid in as precise a way as possible within their cost structures because they believe that their plan participants benefit from such disclosures. We continue to believe that Labor should consider our findings as a starting point for considering whether to require the disclosure of total actual fees paid within its own parameters, including cost to participants. Finally, Labor noted that its disclosure regulations require a statement about the effect of fees over time and a reference to Labor's website where examples can be found. As we state in our report, participants continue to be unaware of the fees they are being charged, which is why we believe it is more useful for the example to be given directly after such a statement, as other nations, like Australia, currently do.

As arranged with your offices, unless you publicly announce its contents earlier, we plan no further distribution of this report until 30 days from the date of this letter. At that time, we will send copies to the Secretaries of Labor, Treasury, and State, the Chairman of the Securities and Exchange Commission, and other interested parties. The report also will be available at no charge on the GAO website at http://www.gao.gov.

If you or your staffs have any questions concerning this report, please contact me at (202) 512-7215. Contact points for our Offices of Congressional Relations and Public Affairs may be found on the last page of this report. GAO staff who made key contributions to this report are listed in appendix IV.

Charles A. Jeszeck
Director
Education, Workforce,
    and Income Security Issues

Appendix I: Objectives, Scope, and Methodology

We were asked to answer the following questions: (1) How are service providers in other countries' defined contribution (DC) systems overseen by regulatory agencies? (2) What key strategies are used in other countries to improve fee disclosure to participants? (3) What key strategies are used in other countries' DC systems to reduce fees?

To answer these questions, we selected four countries in which to conduct case studies: Australia, Chile, Sweden, and the United Kingdom (U.K.). To determine which countries should be used as case studies, we conducted an initial broad review of DC systems in a larger sample of countries. In conducting this initial review, we analyzed relevant nonlegal research and interviewed pension experts to identify 10 countries that had DC systems with key features designed to address fees. Specifically, we obtained comparative and country-specific studies of DC systems published by academics; the Organisation for Economic Co-operation and Development (OECD), whose review also included non-OECD countries; and other industry experts, such as the International Organisation of Pension Supervisors. We solicited recommendations from representatives of the OECD, government officials, academics, industry practitioners, and representatives of industry groups. We then examined the characteristics of each country's DC system for key elements designed to address service providers' costs. From the 10 countries, we used the following selection criteria to select 4 countries for in-depth case studies:

- DC retirement plans are an important pillar of the country's retirement system. By focusing on countries in which the DC system is an important pillar of the retirement system, we increased our opportunity to identify practices used in countries with well developed capital markets and where risks to participants are comparable to those faced by participants in the United States.

- DC retirement plan regulators use explicit strategies to address and oversee service providers' costs. The selected countries as a group should address all of the key strategies we have identified, although no single country needs to address all of them.

- The country was identified through our research and the consensus of external experts as having strong potential for yielding useful lessons for the U.S. experience.

- The country's DC retirement plan is not duplicative. Where similar plans exist in multiple countries, we will select the one that best addresses the other selection criteria.

For each of the four countries selected, we determined how service providers are overseen by regulatory agencies and identified the key strategies designed to improve fee disclosure to participants and reduce fees by reviewing nonlegal research and other available documentation and interviewing officials and industry experts. Specifically, we interviewed industry groups, service providers, and government officials from each country, as well as academics, representatives from the OECD and The World Bank, and pension experts based in the United States. We obtained broad perspectives on the benefits and drawbacks of the countries' regulatory oversight activities and the identified key strategies. Where possible, we attempted to obtain basic demographic data and available data on the types and amounts of fees paid in DC plans in those countries from government officials, pension experts, and others we interviewed. We used these data for the purpose of providing background information and context, or examples, of the effect of certain strategies on fees. We performed some basic reasonableness checks of the data against other sources of information. We did not compare fees across countries because each country, and sometimes plans within a country, can charge different fees; instead, we looked at the types and amounts of fees in each country to gain a better understanding of the effect of key strategies used to lower fees. We did not conduct an independent legal analysis to verify the information provided by or about the laws or regulations of the foreign countries selected for this study. Instead, we relied on appropriate secondary sources and interviews to support our work. Following our interviews, we submitted key statements of facts for review and verification by agency officials in each country and incorporated technical corrections as necessary.

We conducted this performance audit from March 2011 through March 2012 in accordance with generally accepted government auditing standards. Those standards require that we plan and perform the audit to obtain sufficient, appropriate evidence to provide a reasonable basis for our findings and conclusions based on our audit objectives. We believe that the evidence obtained provides a reasonable basis for our findings and conclusions based on our audit objectives.

Australia

Australia

At a glance

Since 1992, Australia has had a mandatory pension system, known as superannuation.

Total system assets: Pension assets totaled about $1.04 trillion USD in 2010, of which approximately 82 percent were in defined contribution (DC) plans.

Coverage: Employers are required to offer a pension plan to eligible workers and provide a minimum level of contributions. The plan may be defined benefit (DB) or DC, but the majority of plans are DC.[1]

Types of plans in the system

Industry-wide or single-employer (28% of private plan assets) The plan is a nonprofit entity managed by a board of trustees, some of which must have equal representation from employers and participants. Trustees must be licensed by the government and are subject to a "fit and proper" test, which specifies certain standards, including experience and educational and technical qualifications.

Retail (34% of private plan assets) A participant deals directly with a for-profit service provider which manages their account. Within the service provider, the plan is managed by a board of trustees. Similar to industry-wide and single-employer plans, trustees must be licensed and are subject to a "fit and proper" test.

Self-managed (38% of private plan assets) A participant manages his/her own account, which entails establishing a trust and a bank account. Up to four people can be in a trust. The participant is the trustee and can select investment options.

Source: GAO analysis of foreign agency documentation and interviews with Australian officials and industry experts.

Pension system highlights

Contributions: The current minimum employer contribution rate is 9 percent of the worker's earnings. The government has proposed to increase this amount to 12 percent. The contribution is required for a band of earnings, which is capped at about 2.5 times average wages.[2] Employers and participants may also choose to make additional contributions subject to a cap.[3] Individuals can voluntarily make contributions when they are unemployed.

Investment options: Most plans offer participants a choice of investment options. On average, retail plans offer 219 investment options and industry funds offer 10 investment options. Participants can choose to receive investment advice for a fee from their plan or from an external advisor. According to agency officials, one-on-one advice can entail high fees and few participants use it.

Default option: Since 2005, employers have been required to designate a default plan for those participants who do not specify in which plan they want their contributions deposited. Australia is in the process of implementing a new set of standards for the default investment option, known as MySuper. Under MySuper, all default investment options must be approved by the pensions regulator and meet standards for diversification and fees. In addition, the default investment options must be unbundled from additional services, such as investment advice.

Leakage: Participants are generally not allowed to access their accounts prior to age 55. When workers change jobs they may leave their account at their previous plan or roll it over into a new plan. As part of the recommendations made from a 2010 review of the superannuation system, Australia is considering implementing a process called "auto consolidation," which would match a worker who is starting a new job to any pre-existing superannuation accounts they may already have.

Drawdown: The minimum age to begin drawing down benefits is currently 55, set to increase to 60 by 2025. The accumulated benefit can be withdrawn as a lump-sum or as an annuity. Most benefits are taken as a lump-sum. Participants over age 55 who are still working may start drawing down benefits. Employers are required to continue to contribute to a worker's fund until the worker reaches age 70, or the worker retires or separates from the employer.

---

[1] The Australian pensions regulator reports that, as of June 2010, 17.6 percent of superannuation assets for entities with more than four members were in DB plans.
[2] Employers are not required to contribute for workers earning less than about $500 USD a mon h.
[3] According to he Australian Tax Office, there is a cap of about $25,600 USD per year on tax deductible contributions for participants up to age 50. For participants age 50 and above, the cap is about $51,100 USD.

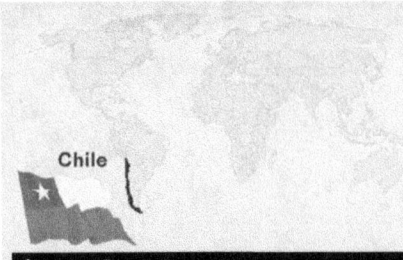

Chile

At a glance

Chile replaced its DB public pension system with individual accounts in 1981. Workers who entered the labor market after that date are mandated to join an individual DC account.[4]

Total system assets: The value of pension assets totaled $148.4 billion USD in 2010, according to the pensions regulator.

Coverage: Workers are required to contribute to an individual DC account. About 60 percent of those employed participate in the system.[5]

Type of plan in the system

Workers can choose which licensed for-profit service provider, known as an AFP (*Administradoras de Fondos de Pensiones*), manages their individual accounts. Currently, there are six AFPs. New entrants to the labor force are defaulted to the AFP with the lowest fee as determined by a bidding process, which takes place every 2 years.

Source: GAO analysis of foreign agency documentation and interviews with Chilean officials and industry experts.

Pension system highlights

Contributions: Workers are required to contribute 10 percent of applicable earnings to their individual account—the earnings ceiling is equal to 67.4 indexed units (*Unidades de Fomento*) of accounts that are equivalent to about 1,500,000 Chilean pesos, or $2,900 USD a month as of December 2011. In addition to their contribution, participants pay fees to their AFP, which currently range from 1.14 percent to 2.36 percent of earnings.[6]

Investment options: Workers can choose between five types of funds, labeled A through E (in descending order of investment risk), offered by each AFP.[7] Each category of funds is subject to limits on the amount of equities that may be held corresponding to its risk level. Participants are subject to restrictions on which investment funds they may hold based on their age. The 2008 reforms created the figure of the pension advisor, a professional who will be able to advise individuals on a range of issues, including the choice of AFP and investment and drawdown options.[8]

Default option: For those who do not choose an investment option within an AFP, the default option is a lifecycle investment strategy in which allocations to risky funds decrease with age (e.g., B fund for workers under 35, C fund for men between 36 and 55 and women between 36 and 50, and D fund for men above 55 and women above 50). According to officials, about 25 percent of workers make an active choice.

Leakage: Early retirement is permitted at any age provided the accumulated capital can finance a pension above a certain threshold. Otherwise, workers do not have access to their account balance before normal retirement age, which is 65 for men and 60 for women.

Drawdown: Upon retirement, participants may choose one of two major options: (a) buy an annuity from an insurance company that pays lifetime benefits; or (b) set up programmed withdrawals with an AFP. Variations on these two options include purchasing a deferred annuity, which means setting a future date for purchasing an annuity and, until that date, making programmed withdrawals from the individual account; or purchasing an immediate annuity with a portion of the funds in the individual account and making programmed withdrawals with the rest of the funds.[9]

---

[4] Additional reforms in 2008 added a Basic Solidarity Pension for individuals with no pensions and a Solidarity Pension Payment for those with low pensions, both targeted to the poorest 60 percent of the population.
[5] This is partly due to the fact that the self-employed (about 25 percent of total employment) were not required to contribute and voluntary contributions for this group have been historically low. The 2008 Pension Reform determines that contribution for self-employed workers is mandatory. The introduc ion of the obligation will be gradual. During the period 2012 to 2014, the default option will be to contribute with the option to opt-out. It will be mandatory for self-employed workers to contribute from 2015 onward.
[6] Each participant also pays a fee for disability and survivorship insurance, which is currently 1.49 percent of earnings.
[7] Initially, only one type of fund was permitted to be offered by an AFP, which was invested in equities and fixed income (current C fund). Since 2000, four additional types of funds have been permitted, ranging from a fixed income fund (E Fund) to an aggressive equity fund (A Fund).
[8] Until recently, plan participants and retirees could get advice from their AFPs or insurance and annuity brokers, but the pensions regulator recognized that this advice may not be considered impartial and objective. Under the current regulations, the names of pension advisors appear in a joint register kept by the pensions and securities regulators, both of which are also responsible for overseeing several aspects of their services. Pension advisors' fees are subject to a ceiling.
[9] For all these pension options, if the worker obtains a pension higher than 150 percent of the minimum pension guaranteed by the state and higher than 70 percent of his/her average monthly taxable wage for the previous 10 years, he/she may use of the sum of money remaining in the individual account as desired (after the calculation of the amount needed to obtain the pension has been made and this has been deducted from the accumulated balance).

Source: GAO analysis of foreign agency documentation and interviews with Swedish officials and industry experts.

Sweden

At a glance

In the mid-1990s, Sweden reformed its mandatory, earnings-related public pension scheme and added a system of individual accounts, called the Premium Pension system.

Total system assets: According to officials, Premium Pension assets totaled approximately $62 billion USD in 2010.

Coverage: Workers and their employers are required to contribute a portion of the workers' salaries to individual DC accounts.[10] Self-employed workers are also required to contribute a portion of their salaries to individual DC accounts.

Type of plan in the system

A government agency, the Swedish Pensions Agency, administers the DC plan and handles recordkeeping for all accounts. Any fund provider licensed in Sweden or registered in their own country can offer funds in the Premium Pension system as long as they agree to certain conditions set by the Swedish Pensions Agency, including a set rebate schedule for all funds, based on the funds' total assets in the Premium Pension system.

Pension system highlights

Contributions: Employers and workers are required to contribute 2.5 percent of the covered portion of a worker's salary. In 2011, the ceiling for contributions was approximately $1,400 USD. Contributions are collected from employers by the national tax authority on a monthly basis.

Investment options: Participants can choose up to five funds from among nearly 800 different funds—at the end of 2010 there were 789 funds administered by 94 different fund management companies and the default fund provider.[11] The Swedish Pensions Agency is currently developing a fund selection tool to help participants make fund decisions depending on, among other things, their desired investment risk. Participants can choose to receive investment advice for a fee from external advisers. According to government and industry officials, because of the large number of investment options, participants are increasingly using these advice services but it can be expensive and undermine the low-cost design of the system.

Default option: For those participants who do not select specific funds, their contributions are placed in a default option called the Seventh AP Fund (AP7 Såfa). AP7 is an independent, government entity operated as a nonprofit with a board of directors appointed by the Swedish government. Since May 2010, AP7 Såfa defaults participants under the age of 56 into global equity funds and shifts the accounts for those ages 56 and older by 3 to 4 percent per year into bonds to reduce investment risk.[12]

Leakage: Participants are not allowed to access their Premium Pension accounts prior to age 61.

Drawdown: At retirement, participants are required to annuitize their retirement savings and the Swedish Pensions Agency acts as the annuity provider for the Premium Pension system. When participants annuitize their benefit, they can choose among two options:

- variable annuity—participants' holdings remain invested in their chosen funds and the Swedish Pensions Agency pays their benefits from those funds,[13] or

- with profit annuity—participants' holdings are sold and moved into an insurance product that pays at least a set amount per year.[14]

---

[10] Employers are also required to contribute to an Income Pension (notional DC) for each worker and may also contribute to supplementary Occupational Pensions (which can be DC or DB plans), but for the purpose of this report we focused on the Premium Pension system.

[11] The default fund provider allows participants to opt into and out of some funds they offer, which are based on risk-levels (cautious, balanced, and offensive).

[12] According to a default fund representative, this high-risk approach was chosen because of the low percentage of participants' overall pension invested in the Premium Pension system.

[13] These annuities do not have a guaranteed value. To calculate the pension for these annuities, the Swedish Pensions Agency divides the value of the account by an annuity divisor (based on estimated average life expectancy) and credits the outcome with an estimated future interest rate minus administrative costs. The Swedish Pensions Agency recalculates the pension amount each year to reflect developments in the value of the participants' chosen funds. For example, if returns in participants' chosen funds exceed the estimated future interest rate, then, generally, the participants' annual pension amount is increased.

[14] However, the participants' annual pension amount may increase above the set amount in any given year.

United Kingdom

At a glance

Voluntary **DC** plans make up most of the private pension system in the U.K. An individual may be a member of a number of different pension plans simultaneously. From 2012 to 2017, all employers will be required to automatically enroll eligible employees into a pension plan— including a new low-cost **DC** pension savings plan called the National Employment Savings Trust (NEST)— and provide a minimum contribution.

Total system assets: According to officials, pension assets totaled approximately $3.3 trillion USD in 2010, of which approximately 40 percent were in DC plans.

Coverage: Individuals in the U.K. can voluntarily contribute to pension arrangements that can be employer-sponsored (DB or DC) or individually arranged (DC). These arrangements are utilized by about half of the working age population, and of those workers only about 30 percent of participants are members of DC plans, including public and private pensions.

Types of plans in the system

Trust-based plans (45% of DC participants) These are employer-sponsored plans and are usually nonprofit entities managed by a board of trustees that typically hire one or more service providers for recordkeeping and investment management services. The trustees are responsible for selecting and vetting the investment options.

Contract-based plans (55% of DC participants) For contract-based plans, an employee deals directly with a for-profit service provider which performs both recordkeeping and investment management services.[15] The service provider selects which investment options are available to the participant. These plans are owned entirely by the worker.

Source: GAO analysis of foreign agency documentation and interviews with U.K. officials and industry experts.

Pension system highlights

Contributions: Employers and workers may make contributions to DC plans. While employers have not previously been required to make any contributions, beginning in 2012, they will be required to automatically enroll eligible workers into a pension plan and provide a minimum contribution. Workers will have the right to opt-out of the plan.[16] The minimum total contribution of 8 percent of qualifying earnings will be contributed to the selected private pension—4 percent will usually be contributed by employees, which is usually matched by a compulsory 3 percent from the employer and a minimum 1 percent from the government, delivered through tax relief.[17]

Investment options: DC plans typically offer between 5 and 10 investment options, but contract-based plans may offer far more than trust-based plans. According to a U.K. service provider, approximately 70 percent of DC assets in the U.K. are in passively managed funds. To choose between the options available to them, participants can receive investment advice from an external advisor.

Default option: When a default investment option is offered to participants within a DC plan, it was estimated in 2009 that 81 percent of members invested in it. All plans used by employers to satisfy their duties for auto-enrollment will be required to have a default fund.

Leakage: Currently, individuals cannot access their private pension savings until they reach the minimum pension age (age 55 as of April 2010).

Drawdown: When employer plans allow it, individuals can continue working while receiving pension benefits. While participants were previously required to annuitize their pension benefits by age 75, as of April 2011, participants over age 55 can now withdraw their pension savings by choosing one or a combination of the following options:

- purchasing an annuity;

- investing their funds in a Capped Drawdown account, which allows them to withdraw up to 100 percent of the value of an equivalent annuity as an income from their pension fund while leaving the remaining fund invested;

- withdrawing their funds flexibly provided that individuals can demonstrate a secured guaranteed lifetime income of at least approximately $31,600 USD per year; or

- withdrawing their funds as a lump-sum when their accumulated balance is very small.

---

[15] Some service providers outsource one or both of these services. Contract-based schemes are owned entirely by the employee, but may be facilitated by the employer. If they are facilitated by the employer, some employers appoint a committee to oversee the service providers' arrangements.

[16] This is the requirement provided that the employee's earnings are above the current proposed auto-enrollment threshold of about $11,800 USD. Employees with earnings below this level will be permitted to opt in to the scheme. There will be a contribution limit of about $6,800 USD a year into NEST.

[17] Qualifying earnings represent the portion of a worker's salary over about $9,000 USD and below about $60,400 USD (as of February 2012). For the first 5 years of auto-enrollment implementation (from October 1, 2012, to September 30, 2017) the minimum total contribution is 2 percent and minimum employer contribution is 1 percent. For the year after that (October 1, 2017, to September 30, 2018) the minimum percentages move up to 5 and 2, respectively. From October 1, 2018, he full 8 percent and 3 percent apply.

Appendix III: Comments from the Department of Labor

U.S. Department of Labor   Assistant Secretary for
                                      Employee Benefits Security Administration
                                      Washington, D.C. 20210

February 21, 2012

Mr. Charles A. Jeszeck
Director, Education, Workforce, and
  Income Security Issues
United States Government Accountability Office
Washington, DC 20548

Dear Mr. Jeszeck:

Thank you for the opportunity to review the Government Accountability Office's (GAO) draft report entitled "Defined Contribution Plans, Approaches in Other Countries Offer Beneficial Strategies in Several Areas" (GAO-12-328). The report focuses separately on enforcement and disclosure. Below, we address these two areas in turn.

Enforcement

In the report, GAO states that EBSA has not yet targeted enforcement efforts based on a broad, ongoing risk assessments, or assessments of key areas of non-compliance with ERISA. Instead, according to the report, EBSA relies on reports or complaints obtained from participants, plan sponsors, the media, and other agencies to conduct targeted investigations, which limits EBSA to leads identified by these sources and not those potential violations that may be more complex or hidden. While acknowledging that EBSA has taken preliminary steps to improve its oversight, GAO found that the more extensive risk-based approaches taken by Australia, Chile, Sweden, and the United Kingdom allow them to take preventive measures and address the short-comings associated with relying on complaints.

EBSA agrees that other countries' experience with DC retirement plan regulation and supervision can sometimes be useful in evaluating U.S. policies and programs. However, GAO's efforts to draw insights for the U.S. from the four countries it examined, which underlie GAO's recommendations, appear to have overlooked important distinctions among our respective systems and governing statutes. Below we highlight some of important differences that exist among the private pension systems of the U.S., Australia, Chile, Sweden and the United Kingdom that the GAO may not have fully considered. These include differences in laws, institutions, and market practices.

1

- The U.S., unlike the four analyzed countries, does not mandate that private employers provide pensions or individuals save for retirement. ERISA only requires that those who establish plans must meet certain minimum standards. Therefore, unlike its foreign counterparts, EBSA must take account of the risk that employers will simply decline to sponsor retirement plans. EBSA must seek to contain retirement plan risk and uphold the law without undermining employers' willingness to sponsor plans.

- In the U.S., pension plans are truly employer-based, and EBSA's authority is plan- and therefore employer-focused. US plans are more numerous than in the other countries, and more widely diverse in both type (ESOP, 401(k), etc.) and detailed features. The other countries' private pension programs are based more in larger, often government licensed or run financial institutions or intermediaries, and are generally less diverse. Therefore it is both desirable and unavoidable that EBSA pursue a wider range of approaches to enforcement targeting (which, as elaborated below, includes risk-based approaches that are suited to U.S. circumstances), rather than a more singular risk-based strategy that is more suited for supervision of a more limited and homogeneous population of institutions.

- EBSA also notes that the other countries' programs generally involve no, or smaller and less discretionary, roles for employers, and arguably tend to resemble U.S. retail IRAs more than ERISA plans. It does not appear that GAO considered this resemblance.

- Along with institutions, authorities also differ. In the U.S., ERISA establishes standards of conduct for plan fiduciaries, who are often the sponsoring employers, but these standards mostly pertain to the care with which fiduciary duties are executed, and therefore leave fiduciaries wide discretion with respect to the specific actions taken. There are no suitability requirements for fiduciaries, nor licensing requirements for plans. EBSA's foreign counterparts generally have more discretion to intervene and require actions as part of supervision of licensed entities, whereas EBSA generally must establish a violation before it can compel action.

- GAO notes that risk-based enforcement is inherently data driven. EBSA's authority to collect relevant data generally is limited by ERISA's provisions governing annual reporting. EBSA's implementation of ERISA's reporting requirements also must take into account the large number of employers affected and the administrative burden imposed on them. Because of these statutory and institutional circumstances, EBSA's data is necessarily less detailed and less timely than the data possessed by the other countries.

2

Notwithstanding these differences, EBSA undertakes a wide range of risk-based
enforcement efforts, most of which we believe GAO has not noted. Although credible
leads from participants, plan sponsors, and other agencies do result in case openings,
EBSA also targets plans and service providers based on historical data, current trends,
and emerging developments around the country or specific to a region. EBSA
continually develops and pursues both National and Regional Projects that target
practices or institutions where particular risk has been identified. Much of this targeting
is data-driven, based on annual report analysis or tracking and analysis of enforcement
data on violations prevalent in types of plans or service providers. Current examples of
national projects include the Consultant/Adviser Project, Rapid ERISA Action Team
(REACT), Employee Stock Ownership Plans (ESOPs), Health Benefits Security Project,
and Contributory Plans Criminal Project. In FY 2011, EBSA devoted 45% of
investigative time to national and regional projects, generating 90% of our monetary
results.[1]

Disclosure

GAO also reviewed the other countries' approaches to participant fee disclosure, again
drawing insights for the US. GAO focuses particularly on counties' efforts to disclose
more complete information on indirect fees actually paid (as distinguished from prices
associated with products available) and the compounded effect of fees on benefits over
time. GAO recommends that EBSA consider these improvements EBSA commends
GAO on the excellent summary of fee transparency activities being implemented in
Sweden, the United Kingdom, Chile and Australia. Although there appear to be
significant differences in the characteristics of retirement plans in the countries GAO
studied, service provider markets, and the applicable legislative and regulatory regimes,
we are open to learn from global experiences that help drive down costs and improve
retirement saving results for workers.

As noted in the GAO report, on February 2, 2012, the Department finalized a new fee
transparency regulation that will provide employers sponsoring pension and 401(k) plans
with information about service provider fees and investment costs associated with
providing such plans to their workers. This final rule, and the companion participant-
level fee disclosure rule which is also going into effect in 2012, will greatly increase the
level of transparency in U.S.-based retirement plans. In fact, we were impressed that the
regulatory approaches in the other countries GAO studied tended to focus on the same
issues that were the focus of our regulatory efforts. Given the multiple year effort and
extensive public input from U.S. consumer groups, employers, plan fiduciaries, financial
services providers, and others that went into the development of our pension plan fee
transparency final regulations, we do not believe it is appropriate at this time to propose
changes to those final regulations.

---

[1] It should be noted that 78% of monetary results are contributed to ESOP project cases.

3

With respect to the specific issues raised by GAO, EBSA notes the following:

- With respect to actual fees paid, the layering and complexity of U.S. market arrangements complicates the estimation of this amount where fees are paid indirectly. After weighing the potential expense to participants and potential inaccuracy of such estimation, EBSA elected to permit such fees to be disclosed as prices in disclosures intended to facilitate participants' choice of products rather than as actual amounts paid (indirectly) in benefit statements. It is unclear from GAO's report whether such complexities exist in other countries, whether the amounts disclosed there are precise or estimates, or what such disclosures cost. Nor does GAO present evidence as to whether such disclosures benefit participants more than price disclosure alone. Nonetheless GAO characterizes such disclosure as an "improvement" for EBSA to consider.
- With respect to the effect of fees over time, EBSA disclosure rules require a statement about such effects and a reference to EBSA's website where examples can be found. EBSA notes that such effect will depend not only on the fees themselves but also on gross returns and on the timing of contributions and withdrawals.

In conclusion, EBSA will consider the GAO's recommendations carefully. EBSA has long participated in multinational pension research and policy discussions and thereby derived insights for consideration in its own policy development. We will continue this activity, with due attention to the present GAO recommendations. EBSA will look into the global experiences described in the GAO report for possible areas of future improvement as we monitor the implementation of our new fee transparency regulations for U.S.-based pension plans.

Again, thank you for the opportunity to review the draft report. Should you or your staff have any questions concerning the statements or requests contained herein, please do not hesitate to contact us.

Sincerely,

Phyllis C. Borzi

Phyllis C. Borzi
Assistant Secretary

4

Appendix IV: GAO Contact and Staff Acknowledgments

GAO Contact	Charles A. Jeszeck, (202) 512-7215 or jeszeckc@gao.gov
Acknowledgments	In addition to the contact named above, Tamara Cross, Assistant Director; Sharon Hermes and Jessica Gray, Analysts-in-Charge; Seyda Wentworth, and Katherine Berman made important contributions to this report. James Bennett, Barbara Bovbjerg, Susannah Compton, Cody Goebel, Kathy Leslie, Ashley McCall, Sheila McCoy, Roger Thomas, and Frank Todisco also provided support.

GAO's Mission	The Government Accountability Office, the audit, evaluation, and investigative arm of Congress, exists to support Congress in meeting its constitutional responsibilities and to help improve the performance and accountability of the federal government for the American people. GAO examines the use of public funds; evaluates federal programs and policies; and provides analyses, recommendations, and other assistance to help Congress make informed oversight, policy, and funding decisions. GAO's commitment to good government is reflected in its core values of accountability, integrity, and reliability.
Obtaining Copies of GAO Reports and Testimony	The fastest and easiest way to obtain copies of GAO documents at no cost is through GAO's website (www.gao.gov). Each weekday afternoon, GAO posts on its website newly released reports, testimony, and correspondence. To have GAO e-mail you a list of newly posted products, go to www.gao.gov and select "E-mail Updates."
Order by Phone	The price of each GAO publication reflects GAO's actual cost of production and distribution and depends on the number of pages in the publication and whether the publication is printed in color or black and white. Pricing and ordering information is posted on GAO's website, http://www.gao.gov/ordering.htm. Place orders by calling (202) 512-6000, toll free (866) 801-7077, or TDD (202) 512-2537. Orders may be paid for using American Express, Discover Card, MasterCard, Visa, check, or money order. Call for additional information.
Connect with GAO	Connect with GAO on Facebook, Flickr, Twitter, and YouTube. Subscribe to our RSS Feeds or E-mail Updates. Listen to our Podcasts. Visit GAO on the web at www.gao.gov.
To Report Fraud, Waste, and Abuse in Federal Programs	Contact: Website: www.gao.gov/fraudnet/fraudnet.htm E-mail: fraudnet@gao.gov Automated answering system: (800) 424-5454 or (202) 512-7470
Congressional Relations	Katherine Siggerud, Managing Director, siggerudk@gao.gov, (202) 512-4400, U.S. Government Accountability Office, 441 G Street NW, Room 7125, Washington, DC 20548
Public Affairs	Chuck Young, Managing Director, youngc1@gao.gov, (202) 512-4800 U.S. Government Accountability Office, 441 G Street NW, Room 7149 Washington, DC 20548

Please Print on Recycled Paper.